SOUL SUR

SOUL SURVIVOR

Gloria Gaynor

with Liz Barr

Fount

An Imprint of HarperCollins*Publishers*

Fount Paperbacks is an Imprint of
HarperCollins*Religious*
Part of HarperCollins*Publishers*
77–85 Fulham Palace Road, London W6 8JB

First Published in Great Britain
in 1995 by Fount Paperbacks

1   3   5   7   9   10   8   6   4   2

A catalogue record for this book is
available from the British Library

ISBN 0 00 627872 8

Printed and bound in Great Britain by
HarperCollinsManufacturing Glasgow

CONTENTS

INTRODUCTION

When I first sang 'I Will Survive', in 1978, I sang it from the heart. I wanted to encourage everybody – including myself – to believe that we could survive. I had had a lot of heartache and suffering, and I thought that I had made it through. What I didn't know then, and so wasn't able to tell anybody else, was *how* to survive, how to get better self-esteem.

It has taken me a very long time since I first sang that song to learn its lesson for myself. In the end I have survived, but not through any power of my own. I have survived because after long years of loneliness, insecurity and lack of self-esteem, I learned to hand all my burdens over to the Lord; and now I survive in His strength.

In the Old Testament, before the children of Israel went into battle, they always sent the musicians out first, sounding the trumpets and banging the drums, to rally the troops and strike fear into the enemy.

If you were to drive early one Sunday morning by the church I now belong to in Brooklyn, you would see hundreds of people on the pavement, standing in line from six a.m., waiting for the doors to open for the eight o'clock service. Even if you stayed and watched while they all went in, another line would immediately start forming for the ten o'clock service; and again, from just after ten, for the twelve o'clock service. The church, which is a converted supermarket, holds 1,100 people and every seat is taken – usually there are more in an overflow tent. When I first joined five years ago there were just over 500 members. Today there are

more than 5000, and the number is still rapidly rising. We have
outgrown the supermarket and are in process of building a new
10,000-seat sanctuary.

Our pastor believes in the ministry of music. I'm proud and
happy to sing in the choir there, and to be a member of a Christian
community in the middle of the poorest part of Brooklyn that
plays the trumpet and bangs the drum and rallies the faithful for
Jesus Christ. Above all, I'm blessed to be learning how to live
happily and victoriously by seeing life from God's point of view.

1

ROOTS

I know almost nothing about my great-grandparents. The only thing I do know is that my great-grandmother was a full-blooded Blackfoot Indian, with hair down to the bend of her knee. My mother and her cousin used to fight over who was going to comb her hair. She didn't want anybody to do it, because she was tender-headed – as I now am. That's all I know.

Her daughter, my grandmother, Fanny Nobles, my mother's mother, was born in Dothan, Alabama in 1899; and my mother, Queenie May, was born in 1914. My grandmother was very young – fourteen – and unmarried when my mother was born, and she didn't want any more people than was absolutely necessary to know that she had a baby out of wedlock; so my mother was brought up to call her 'Sis Fanny'.

My grandmother was very, very strict. She used to beat my mother for the slightest thing, beat her very badly. Today she would probably have been had up, perhaps even jailed, for it. It was virtu-ally child abuse. But I never heard my mother ever say a word of complaint against her.

My grandmother married a man called Frank Smart, and although they later divorced, she would call herself Mrs Smart from then on, and need no longer be ashamed of her motherhood; for my grandmother was a very 'religious' woman, and a great church-goer.

As a child my mother had to go to church every Sunday and every Wednesday, and a couple of other nights a week. On Sunday she would be in church from early in the morning until late in the evening. This turned my mother completely off it. She vowed that when she grew up and had children of her own, she would never make them go to church. And once she left home she did not go, and she did not make us go, and we did not go. Only at Christmas and at Easter could my grandmother talk us into going with her. Her church had a wonderful young people's choir, and we all loved to hear them sing.

My grandmother, however mean she was, however unable to show us any love in a way that made us *feel* loved, was always there. She took my brother Ralph in to live with her when he had to have an operation on his eye. When he was about ten or eleven years old, he developed a weak muscle in one of his eyes and had to have surgery, and afterwards he lived with my grandmother. She made him go to church with her every Sunday. She would listen to Christian gospel music programmes all day long on the radio. Exposed to so much of it, Ralph developed a great love for gospel music which was to influence all our lives later on.

She also took my younger brother, Arthur, and me in once, just for five or six days when my mother had to go into hospital to have my baby sister. My memories of that short time I spent with my grandmother are badly clouded by what impressed me as a child – that she was *so* different from my mother. When you have a mother who only spanks you when even you know that you deserve it; and when you know that you are obedient children, because even the neighbours say you are, and like you, and agree with the way your mother is raising you; and then you stay with somebody who beats you at every turn – it's difficult to have any fond memories. I don't suppose that she really was mean. I guess, thinking back on it, she probably felt that my mother was too lenient with us, and that while we were with her, we were not going to have the freedom that my mother gave us. We lived in a tough neighbourhood, and she was probably afraid for us.

She can't have been all bad because, when we got older and were able to walk the five or six blocks to her house, we sometimes went to see her on our own. Nobody asked us to go, so it must have been pleasant to visit her. It's terrible how I only remember bad things about her. We loved our grandmother – even though I can't remember why!

She was a handsome woman, with a strong face, and skin like black porcelain. I probably look as much like my grandmother as I look like my mother. When she passed away in 1970, aged seventy-one, she had no more wrinkles than I have now.

She dressed very nicely. She and my mother were both – not really fashion-conscious, but wore classic dresses and suits. No-one knew how old their clothes were. My mother made a lot of clothes for herself and for us.

My mother and grandmother never had a loving relationship, but they shared a sense of responsibility, a sort of recognition of, as my pastor would call it, 'right of ownership'. They never moved far apart from one another, and in 1970 my mother and grandmother died a month apart. My grandmother died in February, my mother died in March. My mother had been very ill for a long time and I sometimes think she was just hanging on to get my grandmother safely into heaven before she finally let go of her own grip on life.

My mother knew who her father was, although we children never met him. I called him once, in 1970, just after she died. I don't remember now *how* I found that man! I'd never spoken to him, I'd never seen him, but I suppose I must have found out where he lived from my mother's papers. I telephoned him, and asked him if his name was Moore, and if he had ever had a daughter with Fanny Nobles. He spoke with a really slow Southern drawl, and said her name:

'Yeeah? uh-huh, hm, hm, Queenie May . . . Yeeah – that is my dawerter.'

And I said, 'Well, she passed away yesterday.' I told him she'd been ill for a long time. He just didn't say anything, so I gave him my number in case he wanted to get in touch with me later.

He just said, 'Uh-huh. I see.' And then he hung up. It was bewildering. I thought, well, obviously he hadn't had any contact with her since she was a baby, so perhaps there wasn't going to be any real grief; but surely it must touch you somewhere inside, to know that you've outlived your daughter. He called me back almost at once and said, 'Did you just cawall me?'

'Yes, I did.'

'And you said that Queenie May done di-ied?'

'Yeah.'

'Well, my, oh my. Well, Ah'm so sorry to hear that.'

'Yeah, well – so were we. She was very much loved.'

I told him where and when the funeral would be and all of that, and he said, 'We-ell, thank you-all very much for calling to tell me.'

'I'm your granddaughter.'

'Oh, Ah see! And what is yo' name?'

'My name is Gloria.'

'Oh, Gloria, uh-huh, well, thank you very much for callin' me, dahlin'.' He hung up – and I never heard from him again!

As soon as Queenie May was old enough, at sixteen, she got married. She married James Proctor to get out of her mother's house. And, probably because she had married young and to get out of the house, the marriage wasn't very happy and it didn't last very long. But they had three children, Ronald, Larry and Ralph. Her husband's name was James Proctor, but he was – and still is – called Sonny. Then she met and fell in love with my father, Daniel Fowles, and together they had three more children, my older brother, Robert, who became a Muslim when he was young and now calls himself Siddiq, myself and Arthur, my younger brother.

My mother never said anything bad about my father, or about my grandmother, although I'm sure she must have felt they both betrayed her. She was five months pregnant with me when my father abandoned her. According to her they had the sweetest, most childlike (or maybe I should say 'teenage-like') love affair – holding hands, walking round the streets together, licking off the same ice-cream cone, going to parties and amusement parks, strolling in the evening in the sunset . . . That's the way she described their relationship.

After Sonny, her husband, left, my father, Daniel Fowles, eventu-ally moved in, although they never married. My brother Robert was born. A few years later they were expecting their second child, me, when something strange happened. I'll tell you the story as my mother always told it to me. I know my mother believed it, and because she was my mother, I have always accepted it without question. It really wasn't until I started writing this book that I have begun to question it. This is what she told me happened:

My father belonged to a social club, and one day a woman came to my mother's door and tried to sell her a medallion. She told her that all the men in my father's social club were going to leave their wives and girlfriends. She explained that a young girl had somehow infiltrated the club, even though all the members were men, and she had somehow beguiled all the men and was using 'roots' on them, roots that would cause them to become repelled by and unable to live with their wives. Only the buying of this medallion, the woman said, would undo the power of the roots. Roots are literally just botanical roots, plant and herb roots, but there are certain people who know how to prepare and use them – usually to harm people, to make them physically sick, or to poison their minds in some way …

My mother figured that the woman was just a con artist, trying to sell her a medallion with this wild story, because the woman said the medallion would be the only thing that would keep a man from leaving his wife after having been given the roots. My mother asked the woman how much the medallion cost; when she said it cost a few dollars, my mother laughed and said that my father wasn't worth it. She took the whole thing as a joke.

But sure enough, within a few months, all of the men had left their wives, including my father. All of the men except one – the one man whose wife bought a medallion. And, according to my mother, my father came to her and told her that yes, he still loved her, and probably would always love her, but for some reason unbeknown to him, he was unable to stay with her. And he left.

He always told us he loved her. I don't know if he ever knew about the roots. All of the men in the social club left their wives, but it might have happened anyway – people break up all the time … I suspect now that jealousy and betrayal had as much as anything to do with it.

There are a lot of legends and magical stories about the power of roots, rather like old wives' tales, and like old wives' tales, there's sometimes a grain of truth in them. I think the legends about roots mainly grew up in the Deep South, where both my grandparents came from, their original and daily use, healing was sometimes perverted.

They are often used to harm people and, of course, anybody that's using something to harm another person is doing the Devil's work. But there's nothing spiritual as such about how the roots work. Just as a doctor can give you something to drain the water off your arm, so people can give you roots to make you hold water and swell up. I do know that when you take cocaine, it can change your personality, you can become arrogant, so it's not so difficult for me to believe that somebody could concoct something out of roots to make someone ill, or even to feel repelled by another person.

It is possible that my mother preferred to believe the roots story rather than having to accept the pain of thinking that my father had wilfully betrayed her. She always believed that he loved her, that he was not repulsed by her emotionally or spiritually, and that he didn't know why he couldn't stay with her. I never heard her say a word against him, in spite of what he did.

I'm sure that if you believe something, you can cause things to happen to yourself. Whatever the mind cannot contain, it will impose on the body. My mother believed it, and received it into her spirit, and made herself unhappy and ill because of it.

As I mentioned my mother was five months pregnant – with me. And the break-up so hurt her that she was unable to eat, refused to eat, for several weeks. And I believe that deeply affected me. One thing you will learn about me if you read this book is how so much of what I have done has been motivated by my lifelong insecurity. When my father left my mother, I think I suffered trauma in the womb, resulting in a fear of hunger, because my mother starved herself. I virtually starved in the womb. I hope it didn't affect me mentally! People do say I'm crazy!

I've also been constantly searching for a father; feeling as though there were an aching void inside me, seeing my mother's aloneness and loneliness, and having always had a great fear of loneliness myself. And yet they did have another child. My brother Arthur is three years younger than I am. Although my parents separated, my father still came back to see us. And three years later, because they still loved each other, they tried to reconcile their relationship and, during that time, my mother became pregnant with my younger brother. By then there must have been just too much water under the bridge, because they didn't stay together for long, even after that.

2

150 HOWARD STREET

There was always music in our house.

We all loved it and constantly had the radio going. I would come in for a glass of water, and turn the radio on. If I just walked through the room, I would turn the radio on. I had to have music playing all the time. I remember once my mother took a pencil and wrote on the wall: 'Gloria has just come into the house and left again without turning on the radio!' She said, 'This has to be put down for posterity!'

Sonny, my mother's first husband, played some kind of an instrument. My father played the ukelele, guitar and sang. My brothers all had fine voices, and they used to sing gospel music – one of the effects of my grandmother's influence. Ralph had a beautiful voice, and when he finally came home, after staying with my grandmother he'd listened to gospel music on the radio day and night. He introduced the sound to my other brothers, who all then developed a taste for it. Ralph, Larry and Bobby formed a quartet with a friend of Bobby's called Bakote, and they began to sing – not professionally, just for fun and sheer love of singing. They would get together and sing gospel music for hours.

Arthur was still too young to sing with them, although he'd probably got the best voice of them all. And of course I wasn't allowed to sing with them. I don't think anybody at that time even knew that I had a voice. I was not only too young, I was 'a girl' and therefore I could not possibly be a part of any male quartet. My brothers always treated me like the baby. I became a tomboy trying to keep up with them, but it didn't work. They never accepted me as an equal.

At first we all lived on 15th Avenue, Newark, New Jersey, where I was born; but the childhood home I really remember was on Howard Street, Newark, where we lived for exactly 10 years, from 1 April 1950 until 1 April 1960.

Our house sat behind a three-family house, 150 Howard Street, where my aunt lived. So our address really was 150 *and a half* Howard Street! It was a rough, raggedy sort of a place. We had to walk through number 150 – across the front porch, in through the door, right through the hallway to the back of the house, out of the back door and then across the yard – to reach it. We lived on the ground floor; upstairs there was a husband and wife, who after a couple of years had a child; and above them, in the attic, lived an old man whom we kids always called Willy. We believed he was really old, because he had white hair and walked bent over. He'd smile warmly at us but never spoke, so we never learned his real name.

Our apartment was intended for a family of two. There were eight of us. It had three rooms, which should have been a living room, a bedroom, a kitchen, and a small toilet – it wasn't even a bathroom, it was just a toilet. There was no heat in there and it could be absolutely freezing. One night Larry, aged about thirteen, decided to put the seat of the toilet in the oven to warm it up before he used it. Unfortunately, while he was waiting, he fell asleep and left it there all night. When my mother got up early the next morning she couldn't think what the smell was or where it was coming from. She couldn't believe her eyes when she opened the oven door and there was the smouldering toilet seat! Larry wasn't allowed to live that down for many a long day!

To have a bath, my mother would put a large tin tub in the centre of the kitchen floor and fill it with water heated in pots on the stove. The toilet did have some space in it, so we put one of our dressers in there, because there wasn't a lot of room in the apartment for furniture. My mother had one room, and my four older brothers slept in two sets of bunk beds on either side of what would have been the living room, with an old-fashioned floor-model radio in the middle. In the kitchen sat a chair-bed, which was where my younger brother, Arthur, and I slept when we were really young. When two of my older brothers went into the armed forces we moved into the bunk beds.

It was a nice size kitchen – I wish I had one that large now! It had a pantry and a pot-bellied stove which was quickly exchanged for a small gas range. There were two big slate sinks, large enough to bath my brother and me for the first year or so. And there was a dining set – a table and six chairs. The table could expand to seat eight – it had a leaf. It was an old wooden table with a metal top and a drawer for flatware (cutlery).

The kitchen walls and ceiling were partly papered, and partly made of some kind of metal stuff with squares and designs – it was really kind of pretty – and the floor was wood, covered with linoleum. For us the kitchen was the family living room. My mother kept it very neat and very clean, although the apartment itself wasn't in very good shape.

There was a cellar that we never went into, because it was full of all kinds of garbage that came all the way up to the stairs. We never, ever went down in there. We went down into the cellar in the *front* building, 150, which belonged to my aunt, but for some reason or another, in our house, we wouldn't go down into the basement. Only the man who used to come to read the gas meters would go down.

My brothers were all comics. I felt at one time that I lived with Bill Cosby, whom I'm sure you're familiar with, and Flip Wilson, who's another famous American comedian. Robert, or Bobby, who now calls himself Siddiq since he became a Muslim, looked like Flip Wilson, and told jokes like Bill Cosby; and Arthur had the stature of Bill Cosby, and told jokes like Flip Wilson. But actually they weren't imitating them, they were both just naturally comical. So there was a lot of laughter in the family. People would come and visit us and say, 'You ought to have your own television show!'

My mother cooked for people in the neighbourhood. She was the neighbourhood mother. She was very frugal but at the same time very generous. If somebody was down and out, if a child was put out by their family, they could always come and she'd find some room somewhere for them, slip them in somewhere, let them stay. If children were in trouble with their parents, they would come to my mother. They could talk to her, because my mother had a way about her that was unique.

So there was always somebody eating with us, always an extra person or two at the dinner table, although many times we didn't have all that much to eat. Well, no, we always had plenty to eat, my mother made sure that we had plenty to eat, and that it tasted good (because she was an excellent cook) but she would sometimes only have a quarter to spend. Then she would go out and buy fifteen cents worth of bacon skins and ten cents worth of beans, and get her spices down and her herbs, and make the most delicious hotpot. People would prefer to stay and eat her hotpot than go home to get their own steak or fried chicken or lobster – they loved her beans and her home-made bread. Her bread was flat, because she didn't put any baking powder in it, and it was just delicious. When we were little kids she would make this bread cut into animal shapes. And we'd have our little biscuits galloping round the plate, playing little games. She wasn't strict in that way. You couldn't waste your food, but she didn't mind us playing. She'd say, 'Just eat. Just enjoy yourself.' But she did teach us etiquette. We didn't have a full set of flatware or cutlery but she told us, when we went to someone else's house to eat, to look at what the host did and to copy it. So we had class!

Larry and Ronald were what we call in America 'clothes-horses'. They always dressed in the latest styles. And Ralph too, actually. At first Ralph was a slob. He hated to bath until he was about thirteen or fourteen years old. Then he fell in love with a girl, and she told him that he stank! She really turned him around and after that we all had to stand in line and wait for him to come out of the kitchen where he would be constantly bathing himself in the tin bath!

But Ronald and Larry were always very fashion-conscious, and spent all their salaries on clothes. They looked very much alike, and were always being taken for one another when they were young. They are both still quite fashion-conscious. In later life Ronald used to have big rows with his wife, because on Fridays he'd get paid and, on the way home, he'd buy a red shirt – he loved red, he still loves red. She thought that if he bought a red shirt and got dressed up to go out on his own, he was going out to get a woman! Actually he would just go to the local pub and buy a round of drinks for all the regulars. He had a favourite toast that went like this: If anybody asks who sponsored this toast, tell them, fast talking Proctor from coast to coast.

Ronald is about five foot eight, and very, very thin, because he's ill right now. He's always been a nice size, the right size, the size he's meant to be. He's got a milk-chocolate complexion. Keen features. He's got the best nose in the family, I think. We say he's got a 'white' nose! But a perfect 'white' nose, of course! Kind of thin lips. We all have typical kinky hair.

Larry is heavier. He's about the same height as Ronald. He's got big, pretty eyes and long eyelashes, but he has to wear glasses. Ever since he was a tiny little boy he's had to wear very thick glasses. They make his eyes look small, so you're always surprised when he takes his glasses off by how pretty his eyes are. He has generous lips and a big nose, like my mother's. He has more of a lighter, tanned complexion, and the same kinky hair that's balding now on top. Larry has always had big feet. We used to call him 'Foots' because, from a young age, he's worn a size eleven shoe. He's always been a very good dresser, very neat.

Siddiq is not fashion-conscious at all, and he looks like he isn't fashion-conscious! He's more interested in what he looks like on the inside. To me he's always looked pretty good on the inside! Robert – Siddiq – was my favourite. He's my oldest full brother. He's shorter than the others. He must be five foot seven. He has a round face, very short cut hair, generous lips, generous nose, big, but not too big, eyes. He's lighter complexioned than me, but not as light as the others. He was the most intelligent, the most charming, the most loving, the most funny, just the most wonderful person. He used to tell stories – oh the stories that he used to make up! He had this silly thing he used to do. He'd run into the house, he'd burst through the door, slam the door, and lean his body against it, huffing and puffing and puffing and huffing, and my mother would say, 'What's the matter with you?' He'd say, 'Huff, huff . . . the bear – the bear's after me!'

I thought he was absolutely wonderful. I still think he's pretty neat. He's retired now. A retired presser. He pressed new clothes in factories. He's three or four years older than me.

Ralph is the only one who is ever distant. He was always kind of distant. And stubborn. He's dark complexioned, darker than I am. He also has the keen nose, so it's obviously from Sunny's side of the family. Ralph was and is fat. He got fat early on – I guess in around his late twenties. He and I are the only ones that really have any trouble with our weight. Siddiq, every now and then, would gain weight, but he could lose it again just as quickly.

Siddiq, Arthur and Ronald were probably borderline geniuses. None of them graduated, although that was mainly for economic reasons. It costs money to continue your education. They all left High School and went straight into the armed forces or got other work. But they all got their GEDs. I don't know what it stands for – General Education Diploma, I guess.

Arthur, who is three years younger than me, was the model type in his younger days. He had the perfect model figure. He was five foot ten, wore a size ten shoe, a size thirty-eight suit, and this was perfect. But he wasn't the least bit interested. He also had a wonderful voice, but wasn't the least bit interested in singing either.

For a while he worked with me – as tour manager. One night we were in a theatre, rehearsing, and I went right to the back of the theatre, out of sight of them all, so I could hear how the band was sounding from the back. And suddenly, from out of nowhere, I heard Arthur singing. I could not believe the voice that was coming out of this man! I stood up in the darkness and I said, 'Arthur? I didn't know you could sing like that!'

While he was tour managing with me, I gave him a spot as MC, because he's got the gift of the gab. My mother used to say he could talk the Devil into going to church! He would stand on stage and do a few jokes before the show, and I thought he'd maybe sing a couple of songs, and then announce me – but he *never* sang. He never ever sang.

I think, first of all, that all of our talents were given to glorify God. So, I do believe there are those people whose voices are meant just for God – you know, to stand in the house and sing just to the Lord. Or maybe to sing in a choir. Everybody doesn't have to sing on a stage and be celebrated for their talent. Perhaps he's one of those. Arthur works now with Diana Ross, as chauffeur and bodyguard, and has done since I began so much frequent international travel.

❁

When we were children Arthur and I used to talk from sunup to past sundown, he at one end and me at the other of our kitchen chair-bed. We would wake up talking and go to sleep talking. It was always a wonder to my mother what on earth we found to talk about. But we could talk about anything and everything: 'What are these pot-handles made from? Where do they come from? Have you ever seen the factory? . . .' My mother used to say, 'You know, you don't have to verbalize every single thing that comes to mind!'

My mother was about five foot four, she wore size eighteen, which is actually a British twenty. She was shapely, with very, very fine short hair with grey, like Flash Gordon, just at the top and at the temples; she had nice big brown eyes, a pudgy nose, generous, well-shaped lips, a full brown face, and tweezered, pencilled eyebrows. She was quite well-endowed in the chest – like her daughter – and quite hippy – like her daughter! She also had nice legs – I hope like her daughter – but she had smaller feet than me. She only wore a size eight shoe, I wear a ten (British eight). And she had a really toast colour, the colour of toast. The crust of white bread. And she had lots of tiny little moles on her face and in her hairline that you didn't see unless you got really close.

She was always an 'up' kind of person with a rather laconic, dry kind of wit. She smoked Camel cigarettes for twenty-five years. Ugh! Because she died of lung cancer, I just hate cigarettes altogether.

My mother's best friend was my godmother, Aunt Gee. Her real name is Georgiana Wright. Aunt Gee must be about five foot two. I think she must wear a size eighteen, which makes her even more round than my mother was, because she's shorter. And she's quite well-endowed. She's still quite round, and she's got hair like my mother's, short and fine, and she's another sweet, 'mother of the neighbourhood' kind of lady. She never had any children of her own, but adopted a daughter and her second husband's son.

Aunt Gee had two sisters, Aunt Janey and Aunt Emily. They all used to play pinocle together with my mother. It's a card game, sort of like bridge, and they used to play for hours – I mean sometimes round the clock! They'd get up, take a shower, have a sandwich, sit back down at the table and play some more. I've never seen people who could plays cards the way they did.

My mother told me about one time when she was playing cards and 'cutting' the game. It means that you've allowed friends to come in to your house to play cards, to gamble, and you charge them a percentage of every pot that's won. The police knocked on the door. In those days all gambling was illegal in New Jersey. Only the government was allowed to organize gambling – with the lottery. So the police were in the next room and had to come through another room to get to the game. My mother just took all the money and swept it into her bosom. She sat down and said, 'Not one nickel had better move!'

'What's going on here?' said the police.

'Nothing! We're having a nice little friendly game. Do you want to join us?'

My mother said she was the only one with a big enough bosom to sweep all the money into – and they never noticed!

We had moved into Howard Street on 1 April 1950, and we moved out on 1 April 1960, exactly ten years later, so it encompassed all my childhood. We were poor, but we were happy as the saying goes. Children never mind or even know that they are poor, as long as they are loved, which we certainly were.

We moved, when I was a teenager, to an apartment on the fourth floor of 83 Waverly Avenue, New Jersey, a Government Development called the Stella Wright Housing Project. That remained our family home until my mother's death in 1970.

3

MAMMA'S GIRL

In spite of growing up in a big, happy household, I was a very lonely child. My brothers always treated me like a baby sister rather than as a friend, and the neighbourhood we lived in, in Newark, New Jersey, was a really rough, downtown area, and I didn't find it easy to mix with the other children. I had one best friend, Grear. She is a good friend of mine today, too, and in those days we were inseparable. Mamma used to say that if I had a headache, you could give Grear an aspirin, and I'd be fine! But after a while she and her family moved away, and I wasn't to see her again for over twenty years.

Of course I had a few pals. There was Lester Worthy, whose father owned the shoe repair shop across the street. He used to give us kids old rubber shoe-heels to play hopscotch with. They were the best, because they would land and hold the pavement just where you'd aimed them. Once in a while, if your aim wasn't that good, they'd bounce just once, just enough to move off the line between the numbers, where, if it had stayed, it would have made you lose your turn. There was also Sylvia Bowen, whom most of us were a little afraid of, not just because she was tough, but because she came from a large family, and they were all tough, and known for finishing any trouble that anyone dared to start with their family members.

All the girls liked Earl Johnson! For one thing, he was a good kisser, and for another, he was one of the few guys who would play with us girls. He would play kick-ball with us in the yard across the street from my house, that went fenceless from 151 Howard Street all the way down to the Bowen home at 159 Howard Street! One end of this yard sloped, and Earl would start at the top of the hill and run down with his arms stretched out like an aeroplane. When he reached the ball, he could kick that ball so far and high, it nearly reached the other end of the yard. We girls would all want to have him on our team!

I was a tomboy – not surprisingly with five brothers. I was very, very active, always running, playing hopscotch, jumping rope, roller skating. We were too poor for Mamma to buy us pairs of roller skates, but I had one skate. Boys in the States – I don't know if they do this in Britain – used to take an orange crate, a wooden orange crate, and an old-fashioned roller skate, you know the kind with two wheels at the front and two wheels at the back, and they would separate it, and put two of the wheels on the front of the crate, and two at the back, attached by a long stick. Then they would use it almost like today they use a skateboard. Sometimes they would put another piece of wood like a crossbar on top, and do really fancy tricks on this scooter. That was a boy's toy, but I found one, took the two ends of the skate off, got some yarn, and tied the skate back together again, and I learned to skate like this, with the skate attached by more yarn to my right foot.

I could do such wonderful tricks! I would start off pushing with my left foot, and when I was going really fast I could take my foot up and my body would almost be parallel to the ground. I could go half a block like that. When I finally got the money to get two skates, I could never balance myself. My legs would slide apart and I would do the splits and fall over! It was hilarious.

My fondest memory of my childhood is of my relationship with my mother. She was really my very best friend. We were always very, very close, my mother and I. I looked up to her, I respected her, I probably idolized her. She was the one who loved me, no matter what. I guess she was like that with all of my brothers and later, with my sister, but I really wasn't aware of their relationship with her. I wasn't even consciously aware of *my* relationship with her – it just *was*.

Our mother instilled in us very high morals, but in the form of common sense. Most things she taught us that you did or did not do she taught not so much because they were right, or wrong, but because it was only common sense to do them, or not to do them.

You didn't lie. You didn't cheat. You didn't steal. You didn't do anything that was against the law. She said nothing that you could steal, nothing that you could cheat to get, nothing that you could gain by doing anything against the law, was worth your freedom. And she taught us that eventually you would always get caught. It would not be hidden for ever. Sooner or later you'd get caught. Sooner or later you'd have to pay. And you would realize, by practical experience, that it was not worth it. But it was better to realize it beforehand: from watching other people, from hearing stories about people who had been in jail, from watching television, listening to the radio, reading books, anything rather than learning from first-hand experience that crime does not pay.

I don't know, I can't remember, but maybe she did teach us things about the Bible. She *read* the Bible, but it seemed to me that she read it as if it were a novel.

The real reason why *I* didn't do wrong as a child, was because of my love of my mother. I never wanted to hurt her. I never wanted to disappoint her, because she loved me so much. So when I would go out in the street to play with my friends, and they would decide they wanted to steal pretzels or pieces of candy or whatever from the store – I would not get involved.

When I got a little older, about thirteen or fourteen, the girls and guys would play in the street, and the girls would start running and the guys would chase them, and if they caught a girl they'd get a kiss. I would play, but when they started to go further, I wouldn't continue. The same applied to cigarettes. I didn't want to hurt or disappoint my mother, even if I thought that she would never find out.

The things my mother taught us children, the morals that she raised us with, helped me to develop into the person that I became. She was a very strong woman, raising seven children by herself. There were lots of prostitutes in the neighbourhood. My mother was not one. It was totally unthinkable that she could do anything like that.

I wanted to be *just* like her. I wanted to be talented like she was. She cooked, she sewed, she sang: I cook, I sew, I sing. She had very high morals, and I do. I learned from her – through her morals – an ability to protect myself against doing wrong, even when persuaded by other people. As a child on the street in the neighbourhood, or in school, with friends and peers, I never bowed to peer pressure to do things that my mother had taught me were wrong.

This is another reason why I really didn't have many friends. There was only Grear. I can count the others on one hand and even they weren't really good friends. They were buddies, they were chums, but they would turn on me in a minute. They didn't like the idea that I was the neighbourhood 'Goody Two-Shoes'.

Their parents all liked me – and I could sometimes win temporary popularity by talking their parents out of punishing them; I could help them lie, to get out of things; I was very imaginative, and although our mother taught us not to lie, somehow I learned to be a *great* liar, except to my mother. I could tell a story so close to the truth that, if you later on found out that I was lying and came back to me, you couldn't be sure if I had really told a lie or not.

Then one day, when I was in my early twenties, I overheard my mother, who didn't know I was in the house, talking to a friend in the kitchen. She was saying:

'My children don't lie to me because I've told them that I am not the one to lie to. If you get into trouble, I need to know that I can trust you to tell the truth, because *I'm* the one that's going to help you out of it; but if I don't know the truth, I can't help you. So my children never lie to me – except, once in while, Gloria will make up some fairy story, like "we ran out of gas" when the truth is she and her boyfriend had been out half the night . . . She lies kind of out of respect for my house!'

I was standing there listening and thought, 'And all these years, I always thought she believed me!'

I look back now, and wonder if anybody ever believed what I was saying, or if they all knew and just thought, 'Oh, there she goes again!'

There are stories that I told for years, and I don't know myself any more if some of them are true or not. So I don't tell them any more, because now the Lord has delivered me from lying. I told stories really to build myself up, to make people laugh and to make myself sound more interesting. I thought I was just the most boring person on the planet! Nobody was ever going to be interested in anything that *really* happened to me. I felt that if all the interesting things that had happened to me were written on the head of a pin, there would still be room left for the Gettysburg Address! I used to say, 'Everybody lies when they have to.' I lied to keep the peace, to keep from hurting someone else's feelings, or to keep myself or someone else out of trouble.

Years later, when I became a Christian, I saw a Scripture, in Psalm 119, which says, 'Deliver me from the way of lying'. It really was illuminating to me. I thought, 'I don't want to do this any more' and I really prayed to the Lord to deliver me from lying. And now I don't lie. For me now honesty is not the *best* policy, it's the *only* policy. I've learned that integrity is of the utmost importance if you want to have any peace of mind. And it only comes with learning to speak the truth, with compassion and love.

As a child, I knew that my mother loved me, and when my friends would turn away from me, not want to be with me, when they were going to do something wrong – which seemed to me was all the time – I could always go home to Mamma. I didn't have to do what they wanted me to do.

My friends' parents really liked me; but Mamma, Mamma loved me. And I didn't have to do any of those things. I didn't need those people. I needed them to play with, but I didn't need any backing from them, I didn't need any support from them.

But all the time, I was lonely, and hurt, and afraid of being left out. I wanted to have really close friends, so I tried to buy them, I gave them gifts, things that I really wanted for myself. I realized, somewhere inside, that I really didn't have any friends. There was this sort of tug of war inside me, bouncing back and forth between running home to Mamma who really loved me and would accept me, no matter what, and yet also wanting to be accepted by my friends.

I always came bearing gifts. I remembered people's birthdays. I would give generous gifts at Christmas. This was my favourite time of the year, because I could give my presents without people thinking that I was stupid, or a soft touch.

4

IRMA AND COCO

Unlike the rest of the family, my little sister Irma cannot carry a tune in a bucket with help! She's terrible. Awful. She used to aggravate my mother so. She'd come into the bathroom with this terrible voice, and try to imitate songs by groups. She'd try to sing all the parts, both the lead and the background. She'd stand at the front of her pretend stage to do the lead, and then jump back two steps to do the background, then forward. It was comical but after a while, Mamma would say, 'Please! Somebody come and get her!'

Irma was born after we had been living in Howard Street for a few years when my mother had a brief relationship with another man, Joe Michaels. The relationship – not Irma – was a mistake, no doubt made in a moment of loneliness. Joe never came to live with us, so I never really knew much about him, except he was nice looking and apparently intelligent. Things just didn't work out, but Irma came along in the meantime.

I thought Irma was my little baby doll, my live baby doll, and I took her everywhere I went. It didn't matter to me then if I didn't have friends to be around – I took care of Irma. I took her with me everywhere and showed her off, and she was the one who took up my time. I loved her dearly – as I still do.

So then it was me, and Irma, and my mother. Irma was four or five when Coco came on the scene and, by the time Irma was seven years old, Coco was living with us.

His real name was Clarence Weaver El – you pronounced it Eel. He had been raised as a Moorish American. It's a religious sect but it comes out of North Africa or Spain. They wear these red hats with the tassel. I'm sure you've seen them. Do you remember the film *Casablanca* and the people in the Blue Parrot Café? They were Moors. I think the Moorish Americans are not really accepted by the Moors in Africa. It's a bit like the Black Muslims over here who aren't entirely accepted by Arab Muslims.

We all respected Coco because my mother loved him but I didn't really like him very much. He was very pleasant – so pleasant that I could never have told him that there was anything I didn't like about him. And really the things that were not nice about him were not his fault – they were the result of his upbringing. He would listen to my mother, and try to overcome them.

But I don't like being reprimanded. I never did. I guess I thought I was supposed to be perfect, I don't know. But because of the way he was raised he was very strict, and my mother often had to take him to one side and say, 'Don't raise your voice to the children like that.' We had always been allowed to ask 'Why?' when told to do something, because my mother felt that, if they asked, you should always give children a reason for what you told them to do. It's natural to reject what you don't understand. If you explain to them why, you don't have to keep telling them not to do something, because then they soon learn good judgment for themselves. But Coco, if he told us not to do something and we said, 'Why?', would say, 'Because I said so.' And Mamma would say, 'No, no. That's not good enough.'

Coco was very good with Irma. She got this terrible scalp disease like dandruff, but thick and crusty. It looked as if someone had taken corn meal and sprinkled it in her hair dry and then wet it, and let it dry on her scalp. You could actually lift it up like that. And Coco was so gentle. I could not stand to look at it, and neither could my mother. But he sat down with her with a comb and a brush and some oil, and every couple of days he would just lift that stuff off, and treat her scalp with some medicine that the doctor had given us. Fortunately it didn't affect her hair, and she has always had a thick healthy head of hair ever since.

After I graduated from High School, my sister and I became even closer. It almost seemed that the gap in our ages was closing. She is seven years younger than I am, so we never really got to be pals while I was in High School. I always wanted to protect her. I suppose I tried to help my mother by teaching Irma the things that she had taught me.

Coco stayed with us until after we moved into the Government Housing Development called the Stella Wright Project in 1960. We called him Daddy by then because we accepted him as our step-father, although he never married my mother and was a lot younger than her. I don't know exactly how long they were together but, sometime after we moved into the Project, he and my mother broke up. He had become involved with another, younger woman and my mother made him leave.

So I saw her happy for a few years, but then she was alone again, miserable and lonely. I spent even more time with her at this time.

Irma today is about five foot four inches. She wears a DISGUSTING size five! I mean she's tiny! Sometimes she gets up to a size twelve, but it's never a big twelve, if you know what I mean. You can see that she's put on a little around the middle, and a little in the bust area, but she never really fills out a size twelve. She just wears it because it fits in the waist. But she's tiny, and she's got keen features, beautiful almond-shaped eyes, tanned complexion, and I don't know where she gets her looks from. She looks quite like my mother in miniature, I guess. As a matter of fact I have a baby picture of my sister and a baby picture of my mother, and I don't know which is which!

Irma has always been tiny. There was just one time when I was ever smaller than Irma when I went on a diet and lost 45 pounds in six weeks.

She's got slim legs, small feet, and not high cheek bones, keen features: tiny, thin lips, we call them 'white girl' lips, 'white girl' nose, long pretty lashes, and she's – well, she's got great hair but you'd never know it. She hates to do it, so she keeps it so short, maybe an inch long.

I've always tried to protect Irma, but she won't have it any more. I'd love to protect her, but now she protects me! She's quite a worldly person and she thinks that because I go to church I'm the most inno-cent, naive person, who's never done a bad thing in her life!

So now you've met all the members of my family!

5

LOLO CHOPSTICKS

❊

Being overweight is one of the things I remember from my childhood that has carried all the way through into my adult years.

I only have a very vague memory of being baptized when I was about sixteen. Coco, my stepfather, wanted to be baptized and for some reason I was baptized with him. I know neither one of us was 'born again' and I have only the vaguest memory of the whole incident. I remember slipping in the pool, or nearly slipping, and thinking:

'If I wasn't so heavy, this wouldn't be happening.'

When I was young – up until I was twelve years old – I was always very, very skinny – so skinny that they used to call me 'string-bean', 'skinny minny' and their favourite name, 'Lolo Chopsticks', even though it made me cry. Chopsticks was supposed to describe my legs, which were very long, and Lolo was short for Gloria.

Until I was twelve, all I ever wanted to do was to grow up and to gain weight. I always had a huge appetite; in fact my other nick-name was Cookie-baby because, above all, I adored cookies. I wanted to be big so I could keep up with my brothers; but they were older than me, and I was a little girl, and they wouldn't let me spend much time with them, hard as I tried.

There are stories told about me. I don't know if I have an actual memory of the incidents, or if I just remember them telling me. When I was two years old, the house caught fire in the middle of the night and as everybody was getting out, they came to get me. I stood with my fingers clamped to the door, refusing to leave because I'd found two pennies and did not want to leave until they promised me I could use them to buy some Tootsie Rolls! Tootsie Rolls are chocolate caramel. They look like your finger and they're in three parts like the joints, and the paper is wrapped around and twisted at the ends. I loved them! I still love Tootsie Rolls.

My mother told me that the first lie I ever told was when I was also two years old. She'd gone shopping and left me with Aunt Janey. Whilst she was gone, Aunt Janey opened a box of fig newtons. She'd eat one, and she'd give me one, then she'd eat one and she'd give me one until we finished the box. When my mother came back there was a box of cookies sticking up out of her bag, and I looked up and saw them, and immediately said in a pleading, whiney voice, 'You know, um, Mommy, Aunt Janey didn't give me none of her cookies!' I was putting my bid in for the cookies that were sticking out of the bag. Terrible little girl!

I was very active and could not go anywhere without hopping and skipping and jumping. So no matter how many cookies I ate, I was always skinny. I remember one day a neighbour called to borrow some soap powder. My mother sent me round with it for her and I put it on my shoulder. I was holding it with one hand, and I was hopping and skipping so much that I shook soap powder in my eye. God, it was horrible! I think I might have slowed down a little bit after that.

Round about eleven or twelve little girls start looking at little boys, although the boys aren't looking back. So I started trying to be cutesy. I stopped hopping and skipping and jumping and behaving like a tomboy. At the same time I increased my food intake in a determined effort to gain weight.

With the sudden decrease in activity – looking at boys instead of rushing all around the place – and as my metabolism was slowing down a little bit, it didn't take very long for me to gain a lot of weight. It all happened very fast. To begin with I was really happy not to be skinny any more but nobody seemed to notice, or at least they wouldn't acknowledge it. So I kept on eating until all I needed was an apple in my mouth to look like they were going to put me on a spit and roast me! I was so fat, my cheeks were so fat – it was unbelievable.

Then all at once people started calling me 'fat' – and I was so hurt! To show you how sudden it was, I had a little boyfriend from the time I was six years old. My Aunt Quinnie lived on the second floor of 150 Howard Street, the front building, and she also rented the apartment on the first floor, as we call the ground floor in the States, and used it as a dress shop. She had a customer who had a little boy my age. His name was Lamont and he was my boyfriend as far as I was concerned.

The year I was twelve and suddenly started to put on all this weight, he went away for a holiday, and I think it may have been a few weeks or months before his mother brought him round to my aunt's shop again.

Now my best friend Grear was fat. She had always been as chubby as I was skinny. When Lamont came back from his holidays my aunt called me to tell me and I came running out of the back house, through the hallway. Lamont was standing there, and he looked at me and said, 'You can't be Gloria! You must be Grear!' I was *so* hurt. I don't think I ever got over that. I started the battle of the bulge, aged twelve. I've been dieting ever since.

I love to eat. My mother fed us very well, so you see, it's *her* fault! (I say that jokingly.) Of course it's her fault. It's always the mother's fault when kids are fat. Because when they go away and they think you're going to be upset, what do they say?

'Don't worry, honey, Mommy's going to bring you back some candy.'

And if you're crying because you fall down and scrape your knee or something, then they pick you up and give you a big chunk of chocolate cake and a glass of milk. They always do that. So when you grow up, that's programmed into you: whenever I'm hurt, when someone leaves me, or betrays me, then I deserve to have something really good to eat. So you have cheesecake, chocolate cake or chocolate truffles, and icecream, and you have all that silly stuff, because you think you deserve it – you think you need it, to make you feel better. It's a big lie. A tasty, convenient lie, complete with someone else to blame for your woes.

I really started dieting in the twelfth grade. I didn't want to look fat for graduation. I thought I looked nice. Then something terrible happened. The guy whom I was going to the Prom with got killed, by a jealous girl in New York.

I didn't know him very well and we certainly weren't really close, so the grief was slowly but surely overcome by the joys of graduation. But now I didn't have a date. A friend of mine, Mary, told me that her boyfriend, Cardell, would take me as she wasn't graduating.

My mother made me a beautiful dress. It really was lovely. The background was a pale yellow, with a floral pattern. It had a very fitted, broomstick type skirt and a peplum on the sides, attached to a sash that went around and tied in a bow at the back. The top was very fitted. It made me look ever so shapely now that I'd lost all this weight. My legs looked really nice too, I thought, in three-inch high pumps. My first pumps. I was really in style! I thought I looked fantastic.

I got dressed, and I waited. And I waited and I waited. He didn't come. I called Mary, and said, 'Do you know where Cardell is?'

She said, 'Yeah.'

I said, 'Well, where is he?'

'He's here.'

'So why is he there?'

'He's with me.'

'But I thought he was taking me to the Prom.'

'I changed my mind.'

So I didn't go to the Prom.

It wasn't long after that that I started to put the weight back.

I'm not meant to be like this. I'm meant to be slim, like my father. I never wanted to be skinny, and I still don't. But once – oh so many years ago – when I recorded my first album and they told me I was going to be a star, I decided that I'd better try to look like one. I asked my manager to find me a doctor, and he found me a doctor who put me on a ridiculous diet where I took an appetite suppressant and a thyroid pill to speed up my metabolism. The appetite suppressant made me jittery, so he gave me a little tranquil-lizer to bring me down. I was going up and down and sideways all the time.

Don't anyone be even slightly tempted to follow this. The diet was: a glass of grapefruit juice for breakfast, a glass of tomato juice for lunch and a glass of tomato juice for dinner. Period. And I stayed on that diet for eight weeks. The first two weeks I cheated and would eat a bit of somebody's sandwich; or I would have a shrimp cocktail, or some other tiny little thing. After two weeks I found that if I had anything at all the diet did not work.

I dreamed I saw fried chicken walking around in the yard. Then I had this dream of this humungous – the size of a room – hamburger. And I remember standing way back down in the yard. This hamburger was at one end of the yard, and I was standing back, because when you get away from things, they get smaller. I thought if I got all the way down the other end of the yard, I could get my mouth open wide enough to eat this hamburger. Dreams are so stupid! But after the first two weeks, I wasn't hungry any more, I guess from the appetite suppressants. I was all right. I had a lot of energy. I was working six nights a week, from ten until four in the morning. We were rehearsing – also six days a week – for two or three hours in the afternoon. And I was fine. I slept well at night.

One Sunday morning I wanted to go to church – I had started going to church occasionally by then, but I wasn't very committed, and I hadn't been in ages. I didn't have any mirrors in my apartment, just a bathroom mirror. So I went down to my girlfriend's house, who had wall-to-wall mirrors in her dining room. I went over to see what I looked like and she said, 'Where are you going looking like that?' I pushed past her to see, and I looked like a little kid playing in her mother's clothes! I couldn't believe how big my clothes were!

I'd been wearing size eighteen. The next day I went to the store to get some new clothes, and I tried on a size fourteen, and it was too big! I couldn't believe it! So the first thing I bought was a pair of hip-hugger pants, and a midriff top, to show off these curves that I had not had since I was twelve!

And I kept that weight off – I didn't go back to the doctor. I'd gone down to 138 pounds from 182. I had to renew my entire wardrobe, because there wasn't anything in it I could wear. The next week I went to Bloomingdale's and spent $2500 in about half an hour. What fun! And I kept that weight off for two-and-a-half years until I started to fight with my manager, Jay. When I started having trouble with him and my career, I began to think I should reward myself: again, the big lie that we so often buy. We think 'I'm being good to myself' but we're *not*. Overeating is not going to make you healthy, and it's so unbelievably temporary. The minute you've finished eating, you start thinking about how it's going to make you gain weight, about what you're going to have to go through to get it off again, and you'll already have forgotten what it tasted like. It's just not worth it.

I am one who has tried every diet that ever was, and I know that *every* diet works, as long as you stick to it. The problem is finding a diet that is suitable for you. In the end, most people put the weight back – not because the diet didn't work, or because they've lost too much weight too quickly – but because they haven't changed their regular eating habits.

Adopt a way of eating that's not going to make you feel deprived or bored, or without incentive. When you've got down to the weight that you desire, looking and feeling like you want to look and feel, then you can add a few things to your diet. Now you're on 'maintenance', and this should be comfortable for you for the rest of your life because you are in control.

No matter how you manage to lose weight in the first place, the way to not put it back is to adopt four unbreakable rules:

1. never overeat, that is, never eat until you're really full
2. never eat between meals
3. never eat after eight at night
4. make sure you have six to eight glasses of clear water a day.

If you do that, I can just about guarantee that you will not put weight back on. For two-and-a-half years I ate anything and everything I wanted. If I wanted peanuts or potato chips, they were part of my meal. If I wanted dessert, I either ate less for dinner, a smaller portion, or I left out something. I would have meat and vegetable, and miss out potato, then have a dessert – an ice cream or whatever. I just did not overeat.

In 1986, the last time I dieted successfully, my girlfriend, Lesley Lynch, was getting married to John Sywilok. I wanted to lose weight for her wedding, so she and I went on a diet together three months before the wedding. I was determined that her maid of honour, who weighed less than 125 pounds, was not going to make me look like a blimp. I was weighing 182 pounds, and Lesley weighed 155. Well, Lesley and John both loved sweets and, whenever he would visit her for a romantic evening, they'd sit by the fire or get up on the bed with boxes of chocolate-chip cookies and ice cream. Meanwhile, I was on the diet and I was losing weight, looking more and more gorgeous every day and getting more confident about myself. By the time Lesley got married, I weighed 155 and she weighed 182! But, if you're reading this Lesley, I promise you, you still looked gorgeous!

I am losing weight now, and I am going to get back down to the size where I really feel comfortable and well. And I'm pleased with myself. It doesn't matter what people say when you're feeling confident. But if I get overweight and people say things, it hurts. It really cuts to the heart.

I needed a place of peace and solace and protection from the temptation of appetite and other people eating delicious but un-nutritional foods, whose ill effects can be far-reaching and permanent. I found that place in Christ. As soon as I took it to him. As soon as I said – and meant – that I was ready and willing to be freed from the desire for these things, Christ set me free. It was just as simple as that. As simple as turning my will over to him. All I had to say – and mean – was that I wanted what he wanted from me. Immediately the urge, the inclination, the temptation and even the slightest desire to eat to excess is gone. Whom the Son sets free is free indeed. I call that a miracle and I praise and thank him for it. Hallelujah!

6

FIRST PERFORMANCES

All through my young life I wanted to sing, although nobody in my family knew it. I suppose I caught the desire from both my mother and my father. My father was a professional singer and sang in night clubs with an act called Step and Fetchit, and Mamma had a beautiful voice. She never sang professionally, but she sang around the house all the time.

You couldn't live for long in our house without singing. My brothers sang, my mother sang, even Irma sang. I sang, but nobody paid any attention, or said anything about it.

Although the rest of my family weren't paying too much attention to my efforts to sing at home, I was in the school choir – the Girls' Glee Club, and also the Mixed Chorus, made up of boys and girls. One term we were doing the *Messiah*, and I was chosen to sing the *aria*, with words from Isaiah 7:14:'For behold, a virgin shall conceive and bear a son, and shall call his name Emmanuel, God with Us.'

I remember the thrill of being part of the performance and enjoying the music. The words themselves didn't make any special impact on me at the time. I didn't find them particularly signifi-cant. And yet I think they must have somehow got down into my spirit because, years later, that exact passage of Scripture was to change everything for me, change my whole life round. But that's another story.

After the *Messiah*, a few terms later, I was chosen to do a solo on stage at a school concert. I don't remember the occasion, but it must have been quite a big affair because the Mixed Chorus, the Girls' Glee Club and the Boys' Glee Club were all singing. I was the only one doing a solo. I remember backstage beforehand the others were all saying, 'Aren't you nervous?' and I said, 'Nervous of what?'

'Well, you're going to be out on the stage there by yourself!'

'So what?'

'Well, there are a lot of people out there!'

'What's the big deal? I know them all. I've been at school with them for years.'

They were all amazed at me for being so cool about it because to them it did seem a big deal. To everybody but me. Until I walked out on stage.

I stood in the elbow of the piano. The teacher played the introduction, I opened my mouth and nothing came out. I stood there for an eternity – at least a couple of seconds! – and then she played through the introduction again. I opened my mouth and still nothing came out. I had looked out into the audience and all I could see was a million eyes, all looking at me. I was petrified! The teacher waited a few more seconds, hoping that I would compose myself. I closed my eyes and took a real deep breath. She played the introduction again and I pushed with all my might, and finally started singing the words: 'Only make believe ... couldn't you, couldn't I, couldn't we?'

My confidence grew as the song went on, and I got through it, and I was really good. We were all so relieved! The audience, everybody, including the teacher and myself, were relieved. I don't remember the applause, but I must have enjoyed it.

When the whole show was over the teacher came to me and said something I've never forgotten. She said:

'Look, let me tell you something. When you walk out on that stage by yourself the world is your oyster. Everything belongs to you. Everyone admires you. Everyone wishes it could be them up there, or that they could be you. Everyone wishes they had the nerve to go on stage. *You* are completely and utterly in control. Now you can either hold on to it, or you can give it up. It's up to you.'

I have never had that kind of stage fright again. Every time I went on to a stage in later years I remembered her words, and my confidence just grew.

Of course I do sometimes get nervous before a show, but it's never because I'm frightened to sing in front of the public. I only get nervous when something is wrong on stage: the band isn't right; somebody's drunk; somebody's missing; or my clothes don't look good. If you get a run in your stocking at the last moment, no matter how high it is, when you walk on that stage and somebody in the front starts whispering, you'll *swear* that they've seen the run! It's gone down to your toes, and everyone can see it, and it's all they can focus on, and they're all talking about it, and that's all they can see. They don't hear you singing. They are going home to tell everybody that you were on stage with a horrible run in your stockings! It's ridiculous.

It's not that I walk out on stage thinking, 'Everybody's going to love me'. It's not that. I walk out on stage feeling just like she said – even if you don't sound really great, people are amazed that you have the nerve to go out there at all! My mother used to say, 'Even an angel can't do better than his best!' That's all any of us can expect of ourselves, or of one another.

All I ever hope is that you are going to enjoy hearing me sing as much as I am going to enjoy singing for you.

❧

I gave one performance which I will always remember more than any other. It was at home, when my mother had had surgery on her throat. She had developed a goitre and, after having surgery, she could no longer sing. She would try. She really tried. One day she was trying to sing a beautiful song I was very familiar with because I had heard her sing it hundreds of times. It was called 'Lullaby of the Leaves'. But that day her voice was terrible. She couldn't reach the notes at all. Finally she turned to me and said:

'Gloria, sing that for me, baby.'

Every time I think about it I get choked up, because I remember thinking, 'I didn't know that she knew that I could sing!' I didn't think that she had ever noticed me singing or paid any attention to me trying to sing. And now here she was, asking me to sing a song that I had loved to hear her sing all of my life.

So I sang 'Lullaby of the Leaves' for her, and she seemed to be loving it. And for me, except for the times I have been ministering for the Lord, there has never been a greater audience.

7

FOOTSTEPS

❖

My other first 'public' performance, apart from at school, was when I was thirteen years old. I was singing a song by Frankie Lyman – 'Why Do Fools Fall in Love' – lurking under the staircase in the hallway of 150½ Howard Street, and the lady from upstairs was coming down and she leaned over and said, 'Oh! I thought that was the radio!' And I thought, 'That must have really sounded good! I really can sing!' And that was my first confirmation that I had a voice that could be pleasing to someone other than myself. From then on I decided to be a singer.

My mother was a terrific reader. She was always reading novels. In fact, she read almost anything that was printed, anything she could get her hands on – newspapers, books, box-tops. Because she was well read, people were under the impression that she was a college graduate. Although she made very good use of language and had a large vocabulary she never got past the seventh grade. My grandmother had told her that she had to quit then and go to work to help with the housekeeping.

My grandmother hadn't had much formal education, although she too was an avid reader, and quite well self-educated. She didn't see that anyone else needed any more than that either.

My mother, probably because of this, tried to talk us all into graduating at least from High School and going on to college if we could. There was no money to pay for it, but if you went to work, you might be able to pay your own way through college. After my graduation I wanted to go to college – really to please my mother, of course.

All through High School I took college preparatory courses so that eventually I could study to be a teacher, which was what I thought I wanted to be. I've always been a teacher at heart and always loved children, so I thought that a career in an elementary school would suit me. But although I graduated with honours from high school, I was unable to get the sort of job that would pay my college fees. I hadn't been trained for anything, because I'd been doing the teaching prep courses. I could neither pay my way through college nor get a job. But by then I already knew that college wasn't what I really wanted. What I really wanted was to sing.

My mother was a wise woman. She knew how precarious life could be in show business because she'd seen my father and the struggles he'd had. She knew it was not something you could always count on. She suggested that I should go to a technical school and get trained for some other kind of work, so that I would always have something to fall back on if a singing career didn't work out.

I realized this was a good idea, but I decided that I should try to get into a vocation that I could use even if I did manage to become a singer, so that my time would not have been wasted. So that summer I decided to go to beauty culture school and learned to cut and dress hair. And later I also went to business college, taking a secretarial course and book-keeping.

During the summer after I graduated, my brother Arthur and I started going out to night clubs to listen to the music. We weren't a family who went to church, so apart from the radio, and my brothers' gospel quartet, and my mother herself, singing around the home, night clubs were the only places where I could hear live music – and music was what I wanted more than anything else in life. So that summer, sometimes with Arthur, and sometimes with the girls I met in beauty culture school, I began to experience the night club circuit.

When summer was over, I had found a job at Bambergers Department Store, as a sales auditor. Bambergers is rather like Selfridges in London. It used to be very elegant but these days it's got more junky – or at least the one in Newark that I worked in has. Bambergers was the longest job that I had before my singing career took off. For the first couple of years after I'd left school I had to take several non-singing jobs to pay the rent, like typing, which I wasn't very good at; as well as Bambergers, I worked at Canadian Furs on a Comptometer; I worked at a bank on an IBM sorter and whatever the machine was called that put the numbers on the bottom of cheques. Each job lasted less than a year, some only a couple of months. But in the meanwhile, all the time, I was aspiring and practising to sing.

During my first vacation from Bambergers, I was baby-sitting to help out a girlfriend, and I heard someone walking about in the apartment above me. Someone used to come in every morning at about ten, and walk about upstairs.

Remembering the lady on the stairs in Howard Street, and because I so much wanted my singing voice to be heard, I began to follow the sound of these footsteps and, when they stopped, I would stop and sing. I believed that if I could hear them walking then they could hear me singing. My girlfriend had no idea who lived upstairs, and I had no idea whether it was male or female, although I guessed from the sound that it was a man. So I sang to these feet, and I did this every day for the four or five days I was there.

And it paid off! A few nights later, my brother Arthur and I went to a cinema, and on the way back to the bus stop we stopped outside a night club we knew, the Cadillac club, and the sign outside said that Eddie McClendon and the Pacesetters were performing there. We'd heard they were good, and decided to look in.

While we were sitting at a table with our Cokes, they played a Nancy Wilson song, 'Save Your Love for Me', and I sang along with them – just to myself – because I knew it. Not long after that the band stopped, and the bandleader said that there was a girl in the audience, her name was Gloria and that perhaps if the audience would applaud they could get her up to sing a number or two. I looked around and, to my amazement, I realized they were all looking at me and smiling and beckoning.

I got up, and went, very frightened, over to the band up on the stage. They asked me what I wanted to sing, and since I knew I could sing 'Save Your Love for Me' in the key they had been playing it in, I chose that song. They played it again, I sang it, and we got lovely applause. Then I crept back to my seat with my brother.

When the band had finished playing the set, they came over and asked me if I would like to work with them. I said Yes! I would love to work with them, thinking they meant at some time in the future, or that there would at least be a few weeks of rehearsal, for me to learn the ropes. But they needed me to start the very next night.

It turned out that the manager of the club was the man whose footsteps I had been serenading for the last few days. He had seen me come into the club, recognized me from his apartment building and knew my name was Gloria because one day he'd been coming in and heard my girlfriend call out to me. So, for the second time in my life, someone had overheard me sing and confirmed my desire and belief that I could be a singer.

I was still on vacation from Bambergers, so I agreed to spend the rest of that time singing with Eddie McClendon and the Pacesetters. I was seventeen. I'd had no training, other than the little bit of technique we learned in the Girls' Glee Club at school. But music and singing were in my blood and I wasn't altogether unprepared. Almost from the age of thirteen I had been saving up and buying party dresses, not to go to parties in – I hardly ever went to any parties – but so that I would wear them on stage. I'd been writing in my High School autograph book the titles of songs that I had learned. I didn't know any of their keys, but I had a list of nearly 200 items. I brought this list to the band the next morning and we found suitable keys that were good both for them and me. We spent the whole day rehearsing and then that night I began my first professional engagement.

Two weeks later, instead of returning to my job at Bamberger's, I went with the band to Canada for a two-week tour of clubs and hotels in Ontario. Then we came back to the US, worked in the New York, New Jersey area for a couple of weeks and then, suddenly, there were no more engagements. The band split and I was unemployed.

Bambergers took me back. But in those few weeks of excitement I had been completely smitten by the bug, the chance to sing to an audience, the life on the road and, above all, the great feeling of belonging to a group.

I worked during the day, and in the evenings I would go out with my brother Arthur to different night clubs in New Jersey. We had learned a trick or two by then, so Arthur would pretend that I was this great singer from out of town and tell them that if they wanted him to he might be able to coax me into singing for them! And it worked!

When you start to be successful in show business, people always think you made it overnight, when actually you may have gone through years on what we in the United States call the 'Chitterlings Circuit'. It means that you've made so little money and been so poor, that all you could afford to eat is hog guts! There were lots of clubs that would hire you for one night, or two nights or three nights, and pay you – at the most – say twenty-five dollars for three nights. They mostly took on relatively unknown entertainers, desperate to be seen and heard, which is why they could get away with paying them very little.

I worked for years in clubs with the house bands. I would go in with my book of 200 songs, with the keys that I sang them in, or sometimes we agreed the keys right there on the spot. I always updated my list of songs, so it included the top 40. The band would choose enough songs to get through the engagement and then we'd work. It was a wonderful experience, really wonderful experience. It built character, fortitude and a sense of confidence that you could do this thing, working at your chosen craft.

By the time I was being hailed as the Queen of Disco in the mid-seventies, my publicity machine had swung into action and, *voilà*! the perfect life! The reality is that at eighteen I had just embarked on more years than I later cared to remember of work on the 'Chitterlings Circuit'!

8

THE 'CHITTERLINGS CIRCUIT'

When I went back to Bambergers after leaving Eddie McClendon, I also took on an extra job using my beauty school training at Brown's Beauty World Shop, where the manager, Dolores Newkirk, helped me along and got me customers. It was a happy time and I enjoyed working there very much. The girls and I used to go out together after the shop closed and at weekends.

I still did occasional singing engagements. I didn't have an agent or artist's manager or anything, just word of mouth. Sometimes my brother Arthur kidded the club managers that I was a famous singer from out of state! Don't knock it. People heard me sing, and I got quite a few engagements that way.

And then I got a break. One night I entered a talent contest at the Blue Mirror Night Club and won. Another contestant was Dionne Warwick, whose husband was playing the drums in the band that played for all of the contestants. Dionne went on before me. She's got a wonderful voice and she sang this lovely song. Everybody thought she was fantastic but, thank God, I went on after her.

I wasn't really better than Dionne, but I sang a song that got the club going and that's what they remembered. They'd had the most fun with me. I did it on purpose. I thought I could probably sing as well as she did, but they would remember me if they had a good time. So I sung a terrific song called 'Something's Got a Hold of Me' and they were just boogying down; the whole place was jumping, everyone had a great time and they all remembered that. So I won the contest.

A singer with a group called the Soul Brothers, Bill Johnson, saw me there, and took me down to the Orbit Lounge, a club in downtown Newark. He and his friend Sam sang there nightly, and introduced me to the manager who engaged me on the spot at $25 a week for Friday, Saturday and Sunday nights. So I still kept on the day job!

The Orbit Lounge was a smallish club with a bar in the front and a night club in the back. There was a stage with a band, like a four or five piece band, and a singer and tables and chairs in the back; in the front was an oblong bar and a small kitchen, from which they sold chicken sandwiches, hamburgers and all sorts of fast foods. As a matter of fact, my mother once rented that space and sold food out of there for about six months. I overheard her once talking to a customer who was complaining about the price of her hamburgers. She was her usual forthright self, knowing her hamburgers were better than anyone else's and excellent value for money. I heard her saying, 'I didn't hear you complaining about the price of that thimbleful of liquor that's going to give you a quart-sized headache!'

The Orbit Lounge was a very popular place because it had good live music in the back with the Soul Brothers, and a juke box with the latest dance and rhythm and blues music in the front; so there was always dancing going on in both areas. It was jumping seven nights a week!

While I was working there, Bill Johnson introduced me to Johnny Nash. I auditioned for his record company, which was called Josida – a name made up of JOhnny, SIssy, his wife, and DAnny, his brother-in-law, who all ran the company together. I quit work at both the Beauty Shop and Bambergers to record a song for them called 'She'll Be Sorry'. In Britain there is always someone who knows about this part of my life. A journalist always comes up to me and says, 'I have that record "She'll Be Sorry"!'

The name Gloria Gaynor came from Johnny Nash. My real name was Gloria Fowles but he said, 'That is *not* a stage name. There's no way you can use that name. Why don't you choose a name that starts with a G, so people will call you G.G.? It will stick; it will be like a little affectionate nickname for you.'

So I said, 'That's a good idea. But I don't really know any names that start with a G.'

And he said, 'Well, you know, like Gaynor or …'

And I said, 'That's good!' And I took it. Johnny Nash also encouraged me to start writing my own songs which I have done ever since. So I have a lot to thank him for.

'She'll Be Sorry' was a minor rhythm and blues chart success and I travelled promoting it for a couple of months with Johnny Nash and a couple of other acts that were also on the Josida label: The Cowsills, 'Sam and Bill', and Johnny Day. Then the record company folded and the record died. I was out of work again and came back home.

I knew Bambergers would take me back because they liked me there. But I couldn't face them after having left twice to 'become a star'! I got a job – several jobs – for between one to four months on each job. One was with Benjamin and Johns, one with Canadian Furs again, one at the bank. Then I swallowed my pride and went back to Bambergers for the third time after being terminated at the bank. I had been sent home ill, and while I was away they changed over to a computer system and I missed the training day. They really just needed an excuse to shed unnecessary staff, but I'm rather sorry now that I missed out on learning how to use a computer – it would be useful today! After a short stay at Bambergers my very last non-singing job was with Blue Cross and Blue Shield.

I didn't like working in day jobs. As soon as the singing engagements were enough to support me, I would quit my job. I didn't have a proper agent, but I met a gentleman by the name of Jacky Brown, who claimed to be an Artist's Manager. He began to help me to find gigs. Jacky was much older than me but he was kind, and he could help me. We started to go out and he introduced me to a friend of his, Charlie Langston, who owned a night club called the Front Room Club in Newark. Charlie offered me a weekend engagement, and introduced me to other club owners so that I was kept busy with singing engagements in clubs round Newark for quite a while. I soon realized that Jacky Brown thought he had bought me, body and soul. He was becoming very possessive and jealous. I moved out of the apartment I was living in, and moved back home to Mamma!

Then, at one of Charlie Langston's clubs, I met Cleave Nickerson and the Soul Satisfiers. At that time the group consisted of Cleave on the organ, Al the drummer, George the guitarist, and Sport on saxophone. Apart from Cleave himself we were all in our early twenties. I joined them and we travelled around the New York, New Jersey area and then to a few gigs out of State.

Cleave was a trip! He got us an engagement at the Fireside Inn at Grand Island, Nebraska, in January of 1969. On the way across the country there are loads and loads of Howard Johnson's Hotels/ Restaurants. Howard Johnson's are famous for their ice cream, but they have hotels and, outside of the hotel, across the parking lot or whatever, the Howard Johnson's Restaurant where they served their ice cream and what we call Ipswich Clams. I don't know what they are, but they look long, these clams, and they're breaded and fried. They're wonderful.

And Cleave could smell the place! He would be in a dead sleep, and he'd wake up: 'George? George?' he'd say. 'Is it a Howard Johnson?' (George, the guitarist, was also the driver.) It would be a mile down the road and Cleave could smell it. We had to stop at every one to get him something to eat – every single Howard Johnson across the country. It took us three days and two nights to get to Nebraska.

We were out there at the Fireside Inn for two weeks; when the time was nearly up Cleave called the owner of another club in the area and told him that he was the owner of the Fireside Inn, and that he had this really great group from the East Coast working there. If he wanted to see them before they headed back east, he had better come in pretty soon. The man came and hired us on the spot for an engagement at his club. Cleave called all the clubs in the Midwest one at a time. So instead of going back after two weeks in January, we continued to do gigs in clubs in the Midwest right through until December.

That tour was one of the highlights of my pre-recording career. The American Midwest is truly beautiful, especially in late summer and fall. We worked in Nebraska, North and South Dakota and

Iowa. One area is called the Bad Lands because, although it is extremely beautiful, the terrain is so rocky and treacherous that it is nearly impossible to cross. The mountains seem to be painted with great stripes of autumn browns and reds and golds. We saw where General Custer made his last stand and we visited Mount Rushmore.

While we were out there the saxophone player, Sport, got married and stayed out in the Midwest. He was replaced by Grover Washington Junior who is a brilliant jazz saxophonist and very well known today. In those days we all called him 'Junior'. Then, in December, a storm started up in Denver, Colorado, just as we were setting out from there and followed us all the way back to New York.

When I went home for Christmas and New Year, I found my mother not at all well. She smoked unfiltered Camel cigarettes for twenty-five years and was so addicted that if she was down to one cigarette at bedtime, she would not go to bed. She'd send for another pack and, if all the stores were closed, she'd stand on the porch until someone came by smoking and borrow a cigarette off them to smoke before she got started in the morning. Mamma once tried Lucky Strike, having been impressed by the commercial's claim that they were 'toasted'. Her final word on the matter was, 'they should have fried them, because toasting hasn't done diddly for the flavour!'

I knew all this smoking wasn't good for her. She had seen the doctor a couple of times, but hadn't got any relief or real explanation. Christmas and New Year were very quiet and held very little joy for us, although at that time we had no idea that this would be our last holiday season with Mamma. She was strong and, as sick as she was, she managed to go and attend to Grandma, who had almost completely lost her sight and had to be given daily insulin shots.

The dark clouds began to gather when Mamma got too sick even to do this, and I had to take over. I thought giving insulin shots to Grandma would give me a nervous breakdown. In the first week of February, my grandmother passed away.

Two days after my grandmother's funeral, my mother was taken to hospital. She had lung cancer.

I spoke to the doctor, who said: 'I don't know what your mother's made of, but they don't make them of that any more.'

I asked the doctor if I should stay at home to look after her. I didn't really want to, because there wasn't any money coming into the house for my mother, myself and my sister. He said that it wouldn't do any good, that it would just worry her and he felt that we should not even tell her she had cancer because the anxiety would only make her go faster. He did not know how long she would have to live because he said that, as she had lived as long as she had with so much cancer and only half a good lung, there was no telling how long she would survive.

So I went back on the road with Cleave Nickerson. We didn't go as far this time – just to Grand Rapids, Michigan, where I received, not long after, on 5 March 1970, a phone call from Irma to say that my mother had passed away.

9

MAMMA

Whenever I came off the road throughout my early career, I would open the door, or knock on the door before getting my key and opening up, and she'd come running her little pudgy self, calling, 'Oh, I'm so glad you're home! Oh baby!' She'd greet me at the door. When she died I just missed her. I was too selfish to even think about it being a blessed release for her.

My mother was sweet. She was really sweet. I used to lie on the bed with her, and her arms were fat, really juicy fat. I used to lay my head on them and watch television. It was lovely.

She had more children than she needed, and she had more male relationships than any one woman probably ever wants to have. But, like so many women, she was searching for love that she didn't get from her mother, and couldn't get from her father because he was never there. I quite understand that, having gone through the same thing myself. She was young and hadn't been taught anything about love; and she was naive and ignorant, so she made mistakes. But she was still a beautiful person.

While I grew up being very critical of other people, my mother wasn't critical at all. If I saw something wrong with a person – I mean, in my opinion it was wrong – that their shoes weren't clean, or they had on too many colours, or their hairstyle was not 'in', I would ridicule them to someone else. I'm sure that my friends thought, 'Yeah, and as soon as I turn my back, she's going to make fun of me too.' But I was trying to be funny and was too stupid to realize what they were probably thinking about me.

My mother would only criticize you to your face, and only after the thing she was teasing you about had passed. For instance, if your hair-style was terrible, as she thought, she would not say anything to you or to anybody else. But the next time she saw you, when she thought your hair-style looked really nice, she would say, 'Now! That's nice! That *really* looks good. *That's* the way you should wear it all the time, because the way you had it the other day, honey ...'

I remember her telling my girlfriend one time: 'That lipstick looks so nice on you. You've got lovely lips, and you really ought to use a lipstick like that to show them off, because the lipstick you had on the other day, it made your mouth look as if it was bleeding!'

I would say, 'Oh, Ma! God!'

'But it's *true*!'

She was always very sweet when she was ill, because I think she realized that people don't really want to bother with sick people. But if you're really, really nice, then they'll feel sorry for you and want to help you. I'm very much like that.

I'll never forget the last time I was at home with Mamma and I woke up in the middle of the night. I looked out of my bedroom door, which I had left open so I could hear if she needed me, and I saw her creeping past my bedroom. So I got up and crept up behind her, and I'm whispering to her, 'What are you doing?' She put her finger to her lips and went 'Shhh'. So we were both whispering.

I said, 'What *is* this?'

And she said, 'It's my heart.'

'What about your heart?'

'Every time I lie down, I get palpitations, and I can't sleep so I can't lie down. But I thought if I sneak into the bed, my heart may not know that I'm lying down ...'

She was too much. She was making a joke even while she was having a heart attack. She was really ill, and began to be sick and throw up bile.

She also went slightly crazy in the head. She hallucinated. She went into my bedroom – well, normally she never went into my bedroom, because she always said you needed a road-map to find your way out! – sat on the bed and started playing with her toes.

And she asked me to get her some rum and Coke, which was what she drank. I said 'Uh-uh, honey, you don't need no rum and Coke. What's the matter with you?' And she said, 'I know you think I'm crazy. I'm crazy like a fox.'

So I called the doctor. As soon as he arrived the doctor said that her heart wasn't pumping enough blood to her brain. He sent for the ambulance. She was in and out of hospital within the next six to eight days, and had had a heart attack, a stroke, insulin poisoning and pneumonia. Incredibly resilient!

When she passed away I was keeping in close touch with Irma. We'd talk every evening. We'd spoken that evening, after I'd done a show and was packing up to leave for the next city the next morning. Irma said that she'd been to the hospital, and Mom was OK. But at exactly ten past five in the morning I woke up, looked at the clock, and just started crying and grieving because I knew she had gone.

Irma woke up at five ten. Siddiq woke up at five ten. And Ronald, Mamma's first-born son, whose birthday was 5 March, woke up at five ten. And my mother died at five ten on 5 March.

I was with my boyfriend, a drummer, Al, the Soul Satisfiers' bandleader on the road. I was crying and he said, 'What's the matter?' I said, 'My mother! My mother!' He consoled me and I must have somehow got back to sleep.

At seven-thirty my sister called. I picked up the telephone and she just said 'Gloria ...' and I said, 'I know.' It was a very, very, very miserable time.

I got up, dressed and packed and told the band my mother had passed away and I was going home. They came back to New York later in the bus we all travelled in. I travelled home alone by plane. We lived on the fourth floor of the Project. There were two elevators – an even-floor elevator and an odd-floor elevator. The even-floor elevator was stuck, so I took the odd-floor elevator to the third floor and walked up the last flight.

And as I climbed the stairs, I realized she wasn't there and never would be again. When I went in my mother wasn't there to greet me. Then I did cry.

I had to make all the funeral arrangements. I got together with my girlfriend, Marcia (Marcia, by the way, is the one I was baby-sitting for when I was heard singing by the manager of the club). She was very, very sad, because she was one of the ones my mother had consoled and counselled a lot about her marriage.

I'll never forget one day when Marcia was thinking of breaking up with her husband and my mother said to her: 'Look, honey, if you're going to leave this man, you'd better make sure that that's really what you want to do. Because when your love-jones comes down on you, you're going to have a problem!' Later, my mother and I were going to a store and, as we passed by their house Marcia was going in. My mother sang out gaily, 'Your love-jones came down!'

Marcia and I went down to the supermarket to do the shopping for after the funeral. She said, 'I'm just going to this other aisle' and went off. I came up behind her and she was crying. She didn't want me to see her, probably because she could see I wasn't crying. But although I had cried when I first went into the house, I didn't cry again until two weeks later.

❖

I functioned very well during the time of the funeral. I didn't break down. I didn't cry. I've learned now that when something traumatic happens to me it hits me later on.

My grandmother had had a beautiful church funeral at her Abyssinia Baptist church, where she'd been a faithful member for so many years. But my mother's funeral was not held in a church because she did not go to church and I knew that she would not want to be pretentious. She'd want to be unpretentious right to the end.

They had put a wig on her. She had bought a wig, and someone must have given it to the mortician to put on her. But I knew my mother. She'd probably just been copying me, because I'd started wearing wigs. She wouldn't want a wig on now.

I said, 'No. Nobody ever knew her with a wig. She'd want people to see her, and they'd want to see her, as they knew her.' So I made them take the wig off and I did her hair.

She didn't look dead. She looked like she was sleeping. She didn't even feel like she was dead, not stiff, not hard – she felt fleshy.

It was difficult for me to accept that she had died. I was trying to cry, because I didn't want people to think I didn't care. I didn't think people would understand. I don't know why I was worrying about other people – it must be the entertainer in me that caused me to even care what other people were thinking.

My father was there. My sister and all of my brothers were there except Siddiq. Siddiq felt that he just couldn't handle it, because Mamma and he were very, very close, just like she and I were.

Sunny was there, as was Coco, lots of her friends and my godmother. I went over to the casket, leaned over and said, 'I'm going to make you proud of me.' Then I went away, because I was ashamed that I wasn't crying. I couldn't understand it.

The next morning my sister told me that she and her boyfriend – the nerve of them! – had slept in my mother's bed that night. I was furious. I'd gone to bed and left them in the living room, thinking he was going home. They slept in my mother's bed and turned the TV on; they told me that my mother kept turning it off! It had scared them half to death, and the boy had gone home! I wished she had beat him all the way! But later I realized they were just young. My sister needed comforting and wanted to feel closer to my mother. They hadn't meant any disrespect.

I dreamed that night that I was coming home for the funeral. In our apartment in the Project there was a short hallway, about three feet long, that opened into the living room, and then across the living room was another hallway. The kitchen was the first room off to the right, and my bedroom was the next room to the left. The next room was the bathroom on the right and then the boys' bedroom was on the left. Straight ahead was my mother's bedroom. When you looked into the bedroom you only saw the very left side, and the rest of the room was the other side of the door. As you looked in you always saw her dresser sticking out, and beyond the dresser, against the wall, you could see a small television set that I had bought her to put in her bedroom so that she could watch Perry Mason. She loved Perry Mason. And then later on she learned to love Ironside – who was also Perry Mason. I mean Raymond Burr! She just adored Raymond Burr!

So, anyway, I dreamed that night that, as I opened the door and looked into the bedroom, I saw her shadow on the wall as if she was sitting up in bed. She said, 'Gloria? Is that you, baby? Come here, honey. I'm not dead!'

And I kept having that dream. Night after night after night. Such a disturbing dream. After two weeks I found myself walking down the street at five o'clock in the morning, looking for a drug store where I could get some sleeping tablets. I believed that if you took sleeping tablets you wouldn't dream. I was afraid to go to sleep. The other strange thing is that that was the only dream I ever had about *that* house, that apartment. Any other time I ever dreamed of home, of going home, or leaving home, it was always Howard Street, always the house on Howard Street.

I think the dream meant that I just didn't want to let her go. That's all. After two weeks it stopped coming and finally I cried and I cried and I cried.

10

THE WELL OF LONELINESS

Sometimes I look in the mirror, and I really see my mother. I think she was always lonely, lonely for male companionship. Of course, she was happy when we were young, and the family were all around – I'm sure that any single mother loves her family. But if a woman is alone and has had children it's because they've had a relationship with a man which has gone wrong because they wanted it too much, and have tried too hard.

I know for certain that my mother was lonely just after my father left, and then again from the time that she and my stepfather broke up until she passed away. She had a few boyfriends, but none that meant anything, and she didn't let them come home. She didn't want us to see her with a boyfriend. She said she didn't want to be one of these mothers with all these 'uncles' for her children. The only ones I know of that she had a real relationship with were Sonny, the father of Ronald, Larry and Ralph; Daniel Fowles, my father, who gave her Siddiq, me and then Arthur; Irma's father, but he was only around for a very short time and never came to live with us; and Coco.

By the time Coco left us, my mother was getting very, very sick. She was always trying to diet, because she was overweight, and she developed heart trouble, her back trouble had got worse, she had several strokes, and I spent a lot of time with her instead of going out. I would spend the evenings at home with my mother playing cards, because she loved to play cards.

We would eat peanuts in the shell. We both loved nuts – and coffee – Mamma was an addicted coffee lover and drank two or three pots a day.

I could never beat my mother playing anything. She was a gambler from way back.

My mother and I always maintained a very strong, intimate relationship, but of course, as I grew older, my mother's love was not quite enough. I wanted a boyfriend. As a matter of fact, I wanted to get married.

As I became interested in boys, my morals and my loyalty to the way that my mother had raised me caused me trouble. Other girls in the neighbourhood began to get pregnant. In our neighbourhood girls began to be intimate with boys at the age of thirteen and fourteen, and of course they began to get pregnant. Many girls were pregnant at thirteen, fourteen, fifteen, sixteen years old – and I was a virgin. And because I was a virgin, I couldn't keep a boyfriend.

I wanted a boyfriend, even from the age of thirteen years old. I thought that you were *supposed* to have a boyfriend by the time you were thirteen, you were supposed to go out on dates . . . Certainly by the time you were fifteen or sixteen you were supposed to have a steady boyfriend. And I didn't, because I wouldn't become physically intimate.

So, as before, I began to try to buy *them*. I would buy them gifts for their birthdays – jewellery, cologne, gloves – nothing expensive, but just whatever I could afford out of money I was earning from doing odd jobs, baby-sitting, a bit of waitressing in a fish restaurant, running errands. For a while as a teenager I even did a bit of housework in the neighbourhood at the weekends, because my mother didn't have any money left over to give my brothers or me an allowance or pocket money.

Eventually I did try to keep male friends by becoming sexually active. I wanted to find a relationship that would carry me throughout my life, because I saw how lonely my mother was, and I never wanted to be that lonely.

At first I went from one relationship to another. For about two years I had short-term relationships, less than six months, trying to hold on to men by giving in to their lust, with financial gifts and whatever, and yet it still didn't work. The only time I can ever remember my mother saying something that deeply, deeply hurt me, was over this. It was after I had joined a band, and was dating the leader of the band. Actually my boyfriends were nearly always the bandleaders of whatever group I was working with at the time. This band was missing out on engagements due to band members who would suddenly quit without notice, leaving us without an organist or a sax player or a drummer. This particular bandleader offered to make me part owner if I would help buy an organ and speaker so we wouldn't be dependent on the casual musicians. I agreed, and when my mother found out that I had withdrawn over 200 dollars from my savings, she asked me:

'Who are you buying now?'

I was so hurt. She had never said anything like that to me before, and I didn't realize that that was what I had been doing all along. I didn't even understand it then. I just thought that she had been unkind for the first time in my life. It was only years later, looking back, that I came to realize that she was right, if undiplomatic. I had always been trying to buy friends.

I got pregnant twice and had two abortions. I was told that, when you were less than three months pregnant, there was nothing but blood. Neither time was I having a happy, caring relationship with the father. Once I broke up with one guy I'd been intimate with, had sex with another guy, and didn't really know who the baby belonged to. I didn't want to marry either one of the guys, and neither wanted to marry me. Certainly none asked or even hinted that they were interested in marriage. I was in my early twenties.

For years I've carried the guilt of these abortions, and felt that God was punishing me for them. Even after I became a Christian, I thought that that was why I didn't have any children. In fact, I believed this right up until I was ministered to by a pastor and a Christian psychologist at a Christian Fellowship church in Los Angeles in 1989. They helped me to understand that when I accepted Christ as my Saviour, I was forgiven for all my sins, even the ones for which I couldn't easily forgive myself. Christ died to pay for all my sins. I was free from all the guilt. But I still wish that I had realized, and been told, what an abortion really is, and not done it.

All the while I was trying to find somebody who would love

me, somebody whom I could love. I tried to hang on, to make the relationships work, and the only way I was able to do that was to overlook a lot more. I overlooked seeing my boyfriends with other women – I pretended I didn't see it, pretended I didn't know about it. I became very predictable, very accessible, never went anywhere without my boyfriend knowing where I was and what time I would be back, so I couldn't accidentally catch them out at anything. I overlooked their standing me up, or not showing up until they were hours late. I was always afraid that if I challenged them, they would leave me.

They never gave me anything, and usually the relationship would end by my leaving them, when I realized I was getting nothing back. And this went on until I was in my late twenties. I felt so unlucky in love, I even began to think that God was calling me to be a nun! Friends would advise me that I was too good to my boyfriends. I would say, 'But I've got to be myself. Until I find a man who can appreciate me as I am, I'll keep looking. Changing might make a man like me more, but I wouldn't be happy with myself.' I even wrote and recorded a song entitled, *I Can Take the Pain.*

Which may be quite true in theory, but what I didn't see was that I was *not* being myself, and I was already unhappy with me. What I also didn't understand was that I was looking for something much more than a boyfriend. I was looking for my father. And I was looking for something to fill an aching hole inside me, a yearning for something that I didn't even recognize. I just didn't realize what was wrong, or know how to fix it.

11

BACK ON THE ROAD

After my mother's funeral, I knew I needed to go straight back to work to take my mind off it. I told the Soul Satisfiers I was ready to get back on the road. I found that Cleave Nickerson had been ousted, although it was his band. The other members had got a new organ player called Shelton. I never knew why or how all that came about but I think they wanted us to play more up-to-date music than Cleave did.

The group now consisted of Al, the drummer and the new leader of the band, Billy McLellan, a guitarist to replace George who had had family problems and gone home, and Shelton. Grover Washington Junior had gone even before Cleave left, and had been replaced by Shelton's cousin, Benjamin. Al, Shelton, Benjamin and Billy. We began to work together, trying to find gigs around the New York, New Jersey area.

My sister Irma and I had to move out of the Project, because when you live in a Government Housing Development in the States and your family size changes, then your apartment has to change. There was none to be had in the Development, so we had to look outside.

We moved to an apartment in Lesley Street. By this time I had started going out with Billy. Al had been my boyfriend for a while, but it wasn't really working out. He had threatened that if I quit him, then I would have to quit the band. Billy overheard him. He had seen how nicely I treated Al, and how Al had disrespected and neglected me, and decided that he would like me for himself. So he talked to the other band members and they agreed that if Al wanted to throw me out of the band, they would throw him out. So that's what they did. Billy moved in with Irma and me, to help pay the rent on our apartment.

Al was replaced by Ron, who used to play at the Apollo, and we called the new group the Unsilent Minority featuring Miss G.G. All went well for a while and we had work round the New York, New Jersey area; but then gradually it became harder to find work, and we were all looking for whatever we could find. Shelton and Benjamin finally went back to Connecticut, where they came from.

Then Billy and I got offered a job by Johnny 'Hammond' Smith. He was called 'Hammond' because he was a well-known Hammond organ player. But it meant that the rest of the group couldn't work with us, because he already had a band. He only needed a guitarist.

Billy and I went up to Connecticut to get some pieces of equipment that we had left in storage with Shelton. The equipment had been locked up, and they wouldn't let us take it. Shelton and Billy started to argue. I could see that Shelton was feeling full of resentment, and was smiling with his mouth and not with his eyes. I had an Afro-pick in my pocket, which is a metal hair comb you use if you have an Afro hairstyle, fashionable at the time. I kept my hand round this pick in my pocket and, sure enough, Shelton swung and hit Billy and knocked him for six. When he hit Billy, I lost it! I just went for him. Shelton had a big ring on his finger, and he hit me with it on the forehead. All I remember after that is this big swelling rising on my forehead (to this day, I have a dent there) and the others pulling me off Shelton.

Billy and I began to work with Johnny 'Hammond' Smith. But after only a few engagements, Johnny 'Hammond' Smith said he didn't want me any more, because he said he didn't need another 'star' in his group. When there's a singer out front, it's only natural that people are going to consider her the star. He wanted to be his own star.

I went from job to job, then found work at a club called the Wagon Wheel on 45th Street in Manhattan, New York City, a place with topless go-go girl dancers. A travelling band had called me and asked me to do a one-night stand there with them. While I was there, the club owner asked me if I would like to work with the group that he had there every night of the week, called The Radio because they played Top Forty Radio music.

My sister Irma was working there as a hat-check girl, and told me it was the place to be because all the producers and arrangers and record company people from the surrounding area came in and out – probably because of the topless dancers! So I decided to say yes.

Somewhere between late 1971 and early 1972 I met Jay Ellis Leberman, when he came to see me at the Wagon Wheel. He introduced me to Paul Leka of Columbia Records, who was interested in recording me.

It was the beginning of the seventies. My days on the 'Chitterlings Circuit' were coming to an end. The dazzling decade of disco was about to begin, and I was *never* going to say goodbye!

12

DISCO QUEEN

In terms of worldly success, the seventies was *my* decade. New York City suddenly became the centre of the musical universe and the capital of nightlife, with a host of new stars. I was right up there shining among them!

Jay Ellis Leberman, who became my manager, took me to meet Norby Walters, who became my agent. He hooked me up with a band called City Life, whose leader was Billy Civitella. Billy played drums, Tony Tarsia was bass, Clay was lead guitar, Sal the rhythm guitar, and Gloria Gaynor, singer. We were billed as 'City Life with G.G.' Meanwhile Paul Leka introduced me to Clive Davis, President of Columbia Records.

Clive Davis decided to record me but not, unfortunately, with City Life. It made things a bit difficult between us. They kept saying things like 'If it wasn't for us she wouldn't have got anywhere', which hurt. It wasn't my fault and there was nothing I could do. I signed a contract with Columbia, and I was introduced to Mervyn and Melvin Steel, who wrote my first hit single, 'Honey Bee'.

When it was released, it became known as the Disco National Anthem, because it received so much disco play. City Life and I played 'Honey Bee' wherever we went, and the song became hugely popular in all the disco clubs. Unfortunately, this worked against the record because, although all the disco fans danced to it and loved it, it didn't get an awful lot of radio play. The fans heard it in the clubs, so they didn't need to go and buy the record. It was finally pushed on the radio but by that time it was so widespread and well known in the clubs that it never reached its full potential.

I continued travelling with City Life, and a backing group for whom Jay advertised, after the success of 'Honey Bee'. They were three sisters – Sondra, Cynthia and Tera Simon – who had been working as a disco act called the Simon Sisters. Their brother Linwood Simon had been managing them. I renamed them Simon Said, after the little children's rhyme, Simon said do this ..., Simon said do that ... Jay fell in love with Sondra Simon, the eldest sister, and started managing their affairs along with mine.

We were very busy. Norby got us a lot of bookings, and it was the most consistent work I'd had since I first began singing. We were working all up and down the East Coast, Florida, North and South Carolina, New York, New Jersey, Maryland, and Washington. Shortly after the release of 'Honey Bee' City Life and I were called to work at a club called Fudgy's in Scarsdale, New York, a place we had worked in many times. Fudgy's was quite a club. It had a front, square bar, that you walked into from off the street. The 'show' room was down several steps at the back of the bar. There was a dance floor, and tables all along the walls and, at the weekends, the floor would be so completely crowded with people dancing, or just standing and talking, I used to marvel at how the waitresses could serve them all, and never lose a customer, a payment or a drink! One night a man got shot at Fudgy's. I was on stage and saw it. It seemed to happen in slow motion, as a man was lifted from his chair, up and over the back of it, and the glasses, tables, chairs and people all moved away from him. He was sprawled out on the floor under the table behind. No-one knew what had happened and the man who did it quietly slipped out through the crowd. I saw a glimpse of the back of him, but it had all happened so fast, we wondered if it had really happened at all. We were never questioned about it, and I can't even remember now what the papers said it had all been about.

Fudgy, the club owner, was very keen on making sure his clientele liked the band he hired for the week. If the club didn't like the band the first night, they'd be replaced on the second night; they were often replaced by City Life, featuring G.G. Fudgy's had free admission, and no drinks limit. We usually performed nightly from

10 pm until 4 am, forty minutes on stage, and twenty minutes off. This night we were billed not as 'City Life, featuring G.G.' but as 'City Life, featuring Columbia Recording Artist Gloria Gaynor, singing her hit song "Honey Bee". One hour show, $13 cover charge.' I thought 'My God, this place is usually full on a Saturday night, but tonight it's going to be empty! There's no way these people are going to pay $13 to see an act performed for one hour that they've been seeing performed six hours a night – free! – for the past two years!'

Well, I was never more surprised or flattered, and I've never felt so loved by any audience. The place had a legal capacity of 187, and there were over 700 people there that night. Of course we put together a good show, with lots of new songs, but they treated us like real stars. It was wonderful. I signed my first autograph that night. The young man who asked for it, and I, were both shaking like leaves! I shall never forget it.

We were playing most of the top 40 tunes, and 'Honey Bee', of course, being my record, was one, but we had also started including in our set a new arrangement of a song that I had been singing with the Unsilent Minority, even before I met Jay. I'd been singing it in a rhythm and blues arrangement. The song was 'Never Can Say Goodbye' and ours was a sort of cross between the Isaac Hayes version and the Jackson Five hit, a whole new funky disco version. We were having even more success with it than with 'Honey Bee'.

Meanwhile, Clive Davis had left Columbia Records and moved to another label. I still had my contract with Columbia, but somehow the people who took over Clive Davis' position were not interested in the projects that he'd brought in, and I kind of got lost in the shuffle.

Then, still in 1972, Bruce Greenberg from MGM records heard 'Honey Bee' and decided he wanted the record and the artist. He contacted Columbia, who agreed to release me. Jay Ellis worked out the buying-out of my contract from Columbia so I could go over to MGM. It was very nearly a fiasco. There were endless delays and disagreements about the contract. In the end MGM telephoned at five-thirty one Friday afternoon to say that if they didn't have the signed contract by 6 pm that day, the deal was off. I had to go by foot down to their offices with the signed contract, running all the way from 8th and 55th Street, to 52nd and 6th, and back to 7th, in exactly half an hour! In Manhattan in the rush hour, it would have taken me three times longer by Yellow Cab.

I invited Bruce Greenberg and the MGM President down to hear us performing 'Never Can Say Goodbye', because I was convinced that it should be my next single. I told them that 'Honey Bee' had become a sort of cult hit in the discos but that we were getting as much, if not more, response with our version of 'Never Can Say Goodbye'. That's what got them to come down and listen. They saw that I was right, and they agreed. We did it. And it was a big, worldwide seller, as well as the first disco record ever to be played on the radio.

I continued travelling with City Life and Simon Said but, once again, my recording career caused problems with City Life. 'Never Can Say Goodbye' we played in their arrangement. It had been going over really, really well. Bruce Greenberg of MGM liked the arrangement but, when it came to making the recording, he gave it to an arranger who, of course, wanted a large band – studio orches- tras are usually about thirty-five or forty pieces. So he didn't change the arrangement, he just wrote in more parts. I insisted that the band be allowed to play on the recording, and be given credit for their arrangement, but they had had no experience of playing in a studio, and in fact, they couldn't read music. They also did not understand that six members, as a part of a band of forty musicians, could not play as much as they normally played on stage. So when they came into the studio and were given their parts to play, they walked out.

The record was a smash hit, and has been a hit ever since. People love it, so obviously the original arrangement wasn't messed up. But the band didn't understand that, and I had problems with them from then on. It was really a pity.

In 1974 MGM released the album called *Never Can Say Goodbye*, with 'Honey Bee' as one of the tracks. It was the first album ever to be made of nonstop programmed dance music. It went gold, and I guess it was a milestone in the story of the new kind of disco music everyone was going for.

Almost immediately MGM merged with Polydor and for the next few years all my albums came out on the Polydor label. In 1975 we made the album *Experience Gloria Gaynor*, which made the top 40, and it included a song I wrote myself called 'I'm Still Yours':

> *I've been a lot of places,*
> *I've met a lot of guys.*
> *If one did not have curly hair,*
> *Then he had pretty eyes.*
> *But I don't know what's wrong with me,*
> *I couldn't seem to care.*
> *I just could not accept the love*
> *They offered me to share,*
> *'Cos I'm still yours.*
>
> *I never thought you'd haunt me*
> *The way you seem to be.*
> *I thought that when you let me go*
> *That I would just be free.*
> *But I can't seem to tell my heart,*
> *I can't make it understand*
> *There may be someone else for me*
> *You're not the only man.*
> *I'm still yours.*
>
> *I'm like a slave whose master says*
> *He no longer reigns.*
> *Although you're gone*
> *My heart and my mind are still worked by your chains.*
> *If you can't leave my heart alone*
> *And stop toying with my soul*
> *Then please come back,*
> *You've got my life to mould, to have, to hold,*
> *'Cos I'm still yours.*

Isn't that dramatic!

By then I had gone on 'The Diet' I've already told you about, and lost forty-five pounds. I looked and felt much better, and it got me a lot more attention. Even the band started being nicer to me! It was just in time too because in 1975 I was elected Queen of the Discos by the International Association of Discotheques Disc Jockeys, and crowned in March of 1975 at Club Les Jardins in New York. It was a terrific, glamorous occasion and drew so much international press attention they had to rope off the streets outside to keep back the crowds. I was given the crown and a trophy, and flowers, and I was really pleased to have Simon Said and City Life there supporting me, because it was the biggest thing that had ever happened to me. I was also glad that I no longer weighed 183 pounds!

People wanted to know, but I wasn't telling them, who the tall, bronzed, handsome stranger was with whom I periodically slipped away from the crowds and the cameras to be alone ...

In 1976, I made the album *I've Got You (Under my Skin)*, but it was to be the last album that Jay Ellis had anything to do with, because the next thing that happened was that he and I had a serious falling out.

13

JAY

There's no doubt about it that in the beginning I owed a lot to Jay Ellis Leberman. When he first became my manager he was kind and helpful and took me off the 'Chitterlings Circuit'. I became very attached to him. I knew he could be a bit arrogant, especially in public. When I first met him he didn't have an office or even an apartment in New York. He was living in a hotel and used to meet young artists like myself, whom he wanted to sign up, in cafés and restaurants. We'd sit there for hours, talking, and taking up a table, but only drinking coffee until eventually he'd be asked to leave. He always kicked up an almighty row and swore fearfully whenever this happened, but it happened to him so often he must have known it was coming! We young artists were impressed by his audacity, and found him comical rather than offensive. Jay and I quickly became friends, and I trusted him absolutely. I had lost my mother just a year before I met him and I'd been alone all that time, and now I thought of him as my very best friend.

I had never ever been so alone before. I'd grown up in a big family, and now my brothers and sister had all married and moved away from home. When I was singing with different groups on the road, the bandleader was always my 'boyfriend', and we stayed together. Even if it was only to save money on the hotel bills, I always had someone with me. And I had always been able to go home to Mamma.

Now I was really alone. Once I met Jay, and started working with City Life and Simon Said around the East Coast, I was busy all the time and my recording career started, so I was grateful to him.

By this time I had decided that I wasn't going to have any more of my stupid boyfriends. They had no sense of a future, no sense of who they wanted to be, no commitment to anything, no ambition. I decided that I would sit down and assess myself. I wrote down a list of my attributes, as I saw them, and a list of my faults, as I saw them. I assessed these lists and I decided that this was a nice person, and there was no reason why she should have to settle for just any man that came along. She should have the kind of man that she wanted.

Then I wrote a list of the attributes that I wanted in a man, and a list of all the faults that I could accept in a man, realizing that everyone has faults, and it would be best to have a man with the kind of faults that you could live with!

Then I prayed over those lists and asked God to send me this man, or one as near to my lists as he could find for me if he thought, as I did, that such a man would be good for me! And at that point I stopped dating.

The band would keep introducing fellows to me, and I'd go 'Pff! Nach! Next!' And they'd say, 'Gloria, you're not giving them a chance.' And I'd say, 'They don't deserve a chance! That's not what I'm looking for. I don't need it.' This went on for two years, the loneliest two years of my life. (I mentioned just now that I had prayed to God, and I will tell you in another chapter, called 'Searching', about another thing that was going on in my life at this time. Let's just say that my prayers to God in those days consisted mainly of a list of requests. I had an embryonic faith, but I had not yet come to know the Lord.)

I left my apartment on Custer Avenue in Newark, New Jersey, and moved into Manhattan, into the same building where Jay by now lived and had his office. Even then, when I did come home, I usually slept on the floor in Jay's office, on a mattress from a roll-away bed. I didn't want to go into my own lonely, empty apart-ment.

I had Jay and Norby book me as constantly as possible. Although my personal life was pathetic, my career was really beginning to take off – and so was my weight!

Through the early seventies we were big stars of disco, 'City Life, featuring G.G.', with Simon Said as the backing group. We were earning big money. Disco music was all the rage and everybody wanted us – or nearly everyone ... One place we went to turned out to be a near disaster.

You know how in America we have these clubs and restaurants that specialize in country music? They don't have sawdust on the floor but they are usually fairly basic, like in the old West, with wooden floors, wooden tables with lamps, and a wooden dance floor which is really just a clearing in front of the stage. You'll see the sort of places I mean in the film *The Blues Brothers*, or the Clint Eastwood *Any Which Way* films. City Life, Simon Said and I were invited to perform at one of these country clubs in Maryland. It was a small club in a rural area, but it was known for having good country and western music.

We were the first disco act ever to be asked to come to this club. I don't know why they started with us, because we cost a lot to hire in those days. We had to travel a long way from New York and be put up in a hotel, which all costs money. Really they should have started with some local disco acts to see how they went over but they had made a deal with us, and we had come. They hadn't advertised this fact. The regular clientele knew and stayed away in droves because they only liked country music. The sort of people who liked disco didn't know, so not a lot of people showed up.

The club owner was disappointed, to say the least. When we drove up he was far from cordial. Actually, he was nasty. We set up our equipment and checked out the dressing rooms – which hadn't been cleaned up for us or anything – and it became very clear that this man had a bad attitude.

We went off to check into our hotel and, when we came back in the evening for the gig, the manager was in an even fouler mood. Paul Caldwell, our young road manager, came into the dressing room I was sharing with Simon Said and warned us that we might not be able to go on. He said to us, 'Look, girls, go on getting ready for the show, but be prepared not to perform tonight. This man does not want to pay us. He's telling me that he can't pay us until after the show, and I'm telling him that our contract is for us to be paid before the show, in cash, or with a certified cheque. And he's

telling me that not enough people have come in yet, he hasn't
collected enough money, and so we'll have to wait. The man obviously does not want to pay.'

We had driven down all the way from New York to Maryland.
We wanted to work and we wanted to be paid. So Paul went back
out again to talk to this man and when he came back he said, 'This
man wants us to leave. He wants us to leave *now*. He does not want
us to go on, and he does not want to pay us. And I'm telling him
that he's breaking the contract, and that he has to pay us whether
we go on or not. All he knows is that he expected us to draw a lot of
people and that we haven't drawn the people. And he's got the
police out there! And the police are going to run us out! He's
telling the police that we've treated *him* badly! That we've talked
nasty to him, that we're tearing up his dressing room and threat-
ening him and all that. The police want to come back here and
question you. I've told them that you aren't dressed yet. I want you
to act like you are scared – like this man has threatened you and
scared you.'

So now we're thinking – we've got to be actresses here! By the
time the cops come in I have had this bright idea that if we put
mascara into our eyes, it burns, and our eyes will look red, as if we
have been crying.

But the mascara doesn't work. We have got *great* mascara – it
doesn't burn your eyes! So now our eyes are *black* with all this
mascara we've been putting on. We don't look at all upset – in fact,
we are laughing hysterically! When we see the cops at the door, we
hide our faces in our arms. We're lying across the table with our
heads in our arms, sniggering and laughing, but trying to make it
sound like we're crying.

Well now, the police are *really* concerned! What has happened?
Has somebody hurt these girls? What did the man say? You poor
things! We get all the more tickled, and can't stop laughing. They
think it's hysteria, and say, 'Don't worry, sweethearts. The man is not
going to hurt you. It's OK. We'll take care of everything!'

The cops talk to Paul, and tell him that the man obviously isn't
going to pay, and they can't make him pay, so it's best if we leave and
sort everything out with our lawyer when we get back home. We

gather up our things, leave the club, and drive back to the hotel. Simon Said's older sister, Barbara, lived in Maryland, and had been intending to come to the show that night. We call her and ask her to come and get us so that we, that's her three sisters and I, can go and spend the night with her, leaving Paul and City Life at the hotel with our tour bus.

The next morning, when we get back to the hotel, City Life are standing outside, with their equipment and luggage all loaded on the bus; and the police are there. It seems the club owner has called the police again and somehow got them to believe that we were all liars. The police now aren't a bit friendly and tell us that we have twenty minutes to pack up our things and leave town!

I told them, 'You can have ten of those minutes back!' In ten minutes we had gathered our things from our rooms and were on our way out of town. Maryland was known for being prejudiced against black people, and it was probably worse for us because the band was white, all of the singers were black, and Paul, the road manager, was white. They probably didn't like the idea of a mixed group working together.

Jay took care of all the money. Everybody got a salary, including me, but my understanding was that it was my money. My band and my singers got paid, and Jay made sure that he was like protection for me, to keep people from begging me out of all my money – I was a soft touch – and to keep me from overspending. I never paid any attention to the balance of my books. Money just really wasn't important. As long as it was there for me to spend, OK, and when it ran out, OK, I'd go out and make some more. I think a lot of artists think like that, so stupid.

Jay made some mistakes. But I still trusted him.

When between 1972 and 1976 we all travelled round the East Coast together, City Life, Simon Said and I, Jay would often come too. We were working really hard. I had begun to think that if I was going to be a star I had better look like one, and had lost a great deal of weight. I was dieting, disco dancing, performing and recording, and looking really good.

It was funny, because all the publicity pictures we had were of the 'fat' me, and people would say to me, 'Why are you still using these pictures?' But Jay said we couldn't afford to get any more pictures done.

Sondra, Cynthia, and Tera Simon and I became really good friends. After a while we began to show each other our family photos. I was looking through their album, and I saw a photograph of their brother, Linwood. As soon as I saw his picture, I just said, 'That's the one.'

Sondra said, 'The one what?'

I said, 'The one I'm going to marry.'

And she said, 'Oh! Right!'

I said, 'I'm serious. When is his birthday?' Because at the time, although I was not really into astrology, I did know about the signs and some of the qualities attributed to people of each sign.

She said that he was born on 18 April, which was on the cusp of Aries and Taurus. This was significant to me because my mother, who was my best friend, was Taurus and Jay, who was my other best friend, was Aries, so I thought, 'Perfect! This is the one.'

I felt I was truly finished searching for a man. This was in October or November of 1974, but I didn't meet Linwood until 1975.

14

LINWOOD

I made two more albums for Polydor with Jay, *Experience Gloria Gaynor* and *I've Got You*. They both made the top 40, and sometime in 1975 Jay suggested that I 'incorporate' as a way of saving on taxes. I agreed, as usual without asking any questions, because I trusted him absolutely. But in the meantime, I met the stranger everyone was to be so curious about at Club Les Jardins, Simon Said's brother, Linwood Simon.

Linwood is part Ethiopian and part Seminole Indian. Isn't that exotic? The first time I ever saw him dressed in white I thought, 'This is a bronzed *god*!' The red in him comes out when he gets a tan – because he can get a little bit pale for a black man. He's got this sort of tan complexion and in the winter the tan fades away, but in summer he's positively bronze. When he puts on a white suit, I just fall in love all over again! He's got this jet black hair that's really fine, with fine, tiny, tiny curls, and when it's wet you get patches of curls all over his head. He's six foot tall. He has perfect feet. If nothing else is right in this book, he will love that! He says: 'I'm sorry, but I must repeat, I have perfect hands and perfect feet!' But he really does have nice feet, and he looks good in his shoes. He usually wears wonderful, absolutely marvellous shoes. He is a clothes-horse, like all my brothers, and he loves hats even more than he loves shoes. He is a real 'G.Q.' dresser. G.Q. is *Gentlemen's Quarterly* magazine.

We had an engagement in New Jersey, and Paul Caldwell, our young tour manager, and I had gone over to Queen's to pick up the

Simon sisters from their home. When we arrived the girls were not ready, so I was sitting in the kitchen waiting for them and their younger brother Kenny came in. We sat and we chit-chatted. I'd never met Kenny before, and I thought he was gorgeous. He is still a handsome man, and when he was young he was very, very handsome. He said, 'I'm coming to see the show tonight, can we have breakfast after the show?' And I said, 'Great.' So we made this sort of date.

The girls still weren't ready, and I was sitting waiting, talking to their mother, when Linwood came in. Linwood didn't live there, he had come to visit his father who had been ill. He just walked through saying, 'Hi, Mamma!' and his mother waved at him and he started up the stairs and his mother said, 'Wait a minute. I want you to meet somebody.' And he sort of leaned over the banisters. She said, 'Linwood, this is Gloria Gaynor. Gloria, this is Linwood,' and we both said 'Hi' and he went on up the stairs.

And I thought 'Aha! I know why he came at this minute. He thinks he's come to visit his father, but God brought him in here to stop me going on the date with Kenny.' I told Sondra about it, and she said, 'Give me a break! It's not as if you and Kenny were going to get engaged, you're just going for breakfast.'

I said, 'I would not date two brothers. There's no way.'

And she said, 'Well, what are you going to do?'

I said, 'I don't know. But God brought him in here, and he's going to fix it.'

After the girls and I had all left, Kenny's car broke down, and the only person he could find to bring him to the show was Linwood. We did three shows that night, and in between each show we had a half-hour break. We, the girls and I, would come out and sit with our party – Linwood and Jay, another guy who was Cynthia's boyfriend, Paul and Kenny. Whenever I went over, whoever was sitting next to Linwood would jump up and say, 'Oh, I'm sorry!' and give me their seat. And whenever Linwood came back to the table after dancing with one of his sisters, whoever was sitting next to me would give him their seat as if we belonged with each other.

When the last show was over, I accidentally stood on the hem of my skirt and tore it as I came down the stairs. I thought, 'I'd better do this right now, or I'll forget right up until I want to wear it again.'

So I went back into my dressing room and began to sew up the hem of my skirt. Linwood says that he came to look for me, saw me sewing and I stole his heart! He wondered how anyone could be so celebrated one moment, and the next moment be so down-to-earth as to sit down and sew up her own hem ... I thought that was so silly!

He must have been standing there for a few moments, because I heard the security guard telling him to move along. He said, 'I'm waiting for Gloria Gaynor,' and the guard told him to wait outside with everybody else. He said, 'No, no, I know her,' and the guard said, 'Yeah? How long have you known her?' And he said, 'All my life.'

And I heard this and said to myself, 'Oh yes!'

He said to me, 'I'm driving my sisters home, do you need a ride?' I lied, and said Yes, and waved to Paul to go on without me. So Linwood took us all to his mother's home.

In order to take the girls home, we had to go back through Manhattan, where I lived, but I didn't let him know it. So we arrived at their home, and went in and chatted for a bit. By now it was two, two-thirty in the morning, and one of the girls' boyfriends asked Linwood if he could give him a ride home. Before Linwood could answer I jumped up and said, 'Well, I think I'm going to make some pancakes. Anybody else want any pancakes? Anybody hungry?'

I had never cooked in their house before. I think I'd only ever been there once. But I started looking in the refrigerator, and Sondra and I began to make breakfast and Linwood said to the other guy, 'No, man, I'm going to wait for these pancakes.' So the boyfriend left, and we all ate breakfast.

Then Kenny asked Linwood to take him home. Until this moment I had completely forgotten Kenny and our date! I mean he was there, and I'd been talking to him like to everyone else, but I just forgot that I was supposed to be going out to breakfast with him that morning.

I was determined to keep Linwood there as long as I could – which was why I had started cooking pancakes – but when Kenny asked Linwood for a ride, I knew I couldn't hold him any longer. But Linwood turned to me, and asked me if I wanted to ride with him.

Driving back again from Kenny's house, we were both talking and talking. We both stopped at the same moment and said, 'Am I talking too much?' And we both said No together. And then there was silence for a few minutes, and then he took my hand. We were holding hands on the seat between us, and I realized that he wasn't driving towards his mother's house in Queen's.

He said, 'I have a night club. I thought you might like to see it.'

I said, 'A night club? At four o'clock in the morning? It must be closed now.'

'Yeah. But it's my club. I'll open it.'

We went to Brooklyn and he opened the club. He turned on the lights, and the disco lights and the music, and poured us two glasses of Harvey's Bristol Cream, and we danced. It was just marvellous. I was in heaven. We danced and then we'd stop and talk, and then dance some more, and talk some more.

When we left I noticed that again we weren't going towards his mother's house. This time I didn't say anything, I just waited to see what he was going to do. I had purposely left my handbag at his mother's house, because I had wanted him not to be able to take me straight home from his brother's. I wanted him to have to go back, to have that much more time with him.

He drove to the beach at Coney Island, New York, and we watched the sun rise. I thought, 'Oh! This is my man. He is too much.' He was so handsome, and so regal looking. Kenny was a nice looking boy, but Linwood was a man. He danced really well, and he was a gentleman, and treated everybody nicely, and he spoke really well, and now I found that he was also a romantic. He was wonderful.

Before we finally parted, when he was driving off, he looked at me and said, 'Do you know what?'

I said, 'What?' He said, 'I think we're going to be together for the rest of our lives.'

I said, 'You know what? I think so too.'

I let myself into my apartment, and like in the movies, I just fell back against my door, heaved a sigh, had wonderful dreams. I was utterly convinced that, as he said, I had at last found the man I was going to be with for the rest of my life.

❀

Linwood warned me about Jay but I didn't take much notice of him. I would sign whatever Jay stuck under my nose. One day we were going off on the road, and Linwood was taking me in his car, and everybody else was going on the tour bus. When Jay came down to the car with some papers for me to sign, I signed them, and he went back into his office. Linwood said, 'What was that?'

And I looked at him as if to say 'none of your business', but said, 'Why?'

He said, 'Well, I mean, it was the way you signed them. Did you know what they were?'

And I said, 'Er? er? No. I don't know what they were. It's not important.'

So he said, 'What do you mean, it's not important? You just sign stuff, you don't even know what you are signing?'

I said, 'Well, Jay's my friend! He's not going to have me sign anything that's going to hurt me.'

He said, 'Well that's probably true, but there is such a thing as conflict of interest. He has a lawyer, who makes sure that he does what's good for him. You should have one too.' I knew he was right but I really didn't pay too much attention to it.

❀

I had started appearing on American television shows, and as a result I *nearly* went out on a date with George Foreman! I appeared on Don Kershner's Rock Concert, and George Foreman must have been watching, because he sent someone round to ask me if I would go out with him. I had to tell you this, because I think George Foreman is absolutely wonderful! I don't know if he's got five or six sons now, but they are all christened George! Isn't that crazy? But anyway, I was madly in love with Linwood by this time, so I turned George down. I must have been in love!

❀

Jay had found out that Linwood knew about the business. He had successfully managed his sisters, and had been a New York Port Authority policeman for about eight years when I first met him. Jay had never minded me having a boyfriend before, because he knew my boyfriends were all rubbish. But when I started going out with Linwood, his attitude began to change towards me. He got scared. He even tried to frame Linwood on a totally ridiculous, trumped-up robbery charge. He asked Linwood to go to his office one day and collect some papers he'd left behind on his desk. Later, Jay accused Linwood of stealing a few hundred dollars from the office safe. What he didn't know was that when Linwood had gone inside the building he had run into Jay's partner, and he, not Linwood, had gone into the office to pick up the papers. That made Jay even more furious.

After my conversation with Linwood, and particularly after this sign of Jay becoming hostile, I went to Jay and said: 'I want to know what this corporation thing is all about. I really don't understand.'

He said, 'Why don't you ask the lawyer? You're going to Venezuela in a couple of weeks, and he'll be going with you, so you can ask him then.'

This lawyer was Jay's lawyer, but I thought he was supposed to be *our* lawyer, because I didn't understand that a manager and an artist ought to have separate lawyers. I thought it was *our* corporation, primarily mine, but Jay was running it.

So on the trip in question I asked the lawyer about it, and he said, 'I can't really tell you, because I'm Jay's lawyer, and it would be unethical for me to counsel you.'

I said, 'Oh! I thought you were *our* lawyer.'

He said, 'Oh no, I can't counsel both of you, because there's a conflict of interest,' which was just what Linwood had said. Then the lawyer said, 'But it is your corporation. I've got the corporate kit, and whenever you want you can come and get it and take it to your own lawyer, and he can explain it.'

Linwood was with us, and I told him what the lawyer had said, and he said, 'So when we get back to New York, I'll get you a lawyer.'

When we got back to New York, I asked Jay's lawyer for the

corporation kit to take to my own lawyer. I took it away with me, but no sooner had I opened the door of my apartment when the telephone rang. It was Jay.

Now Jay had never spoken to me before in a derogatory way. I'd heard him use foul language, but never at me. But now he was calling me the most terrible names: 'You slimey, M-F BITCH, you bring your so-and-so down here right now.'

I was thinking, 'What on earth is wrong with him?' I went down to his office, and there was a guy whom I knew to be a member of an organized crime family. I don't know if Jay had ever actually told me, but it had been my impression that he was associated in some way with these people. And when I saw this guy sitting there, I got scared.

Jay continued calling me all these names, and telling me that he would see me in the gutter. How dared I go to his lawyer and ask him questions about him? I said, 'I never asked him anything about you. I simply got my corporate kit, which he told me I was at liberty to do, and that I could take it to somebody to explain to me what it was all about.'

Jay picked up the telephone and pretended that he was talking to the record company. He said they might as well tear up my contract, because I would never be recording again. I thought it was for real. Then he said he was calling our agency, and told them to cancel all of my contracts, because I would not be honouring any of them.

I had sense enough to know that he could not cancel a forth-coming trip to Brazil. But I was terrified because he was saying all these things in front of this stranger, and I thought Jay had got him there as a threat. So I was trembling in my boots. But I was getting angry too. It was obvious to me that what all this was about was money. I said, 'Well, if you want a fight, you got a fight. But do you know something? Just as it's easier to do something when you don't have to do it, it's also easier to have something when you don't have to have it. And I don't have to have money – you do. So I'm going to win this fight.'

He asked me for the corporation kit, but I said I'd already taken it to my lawyer. I walked out and went back to my apartment. As soon as it was time for Linwood to be clocking in at work, I called him, and told him what had happened. He told me to call the lawyer, who sent a messenger round to collect the kit. He told me to put in an envelope any other papers that I didn't want Jay to get hold of, so I did.

We went through terrible fights about breaking the contract. Jay tried to sue Linwood for five million dollars for contractual interference. I didn't have any contract with Linwood, so Jay couldn't prove a thing. We didn't even have a verbal agreement. Then Jay tried to file a suit against Linwood in the name of his sisters – they said they didn't know anything about it – for another five million dollars, and he sued me again for five million dollars that I had some girls on stage pretending to be Simon Said. He had really lost it.

That night, after I'd sent the letters and corporation kit and everything to the lawyer, I called my tour manager, Paul Caldwell. He was a lovely, lovely young man, gay, the youngest member of the group, but the most respected. He was on call twenty-four hours a day. He would do anything and everything for us. He would go on errands, he would iron clothes, cook food, just anything we wanted. He took care of the books and the business, made sure everything went on on time, checked the stage, made sure we had everything we needed. He was wonderful. I loved him, and he loved me.

I told him Jay was furious. He said, 'I know. He's called me and said we're not going to Brazil. And he's called the band and the girls and told them too.'

I said, 'Oh yes, we are going to Brazil. I have that contract. And even if I didn't have it, the people in Brazil have their copy.'

Paul told me Jay had locked up our clothes and equipment.

I said, 'Those aren't the only clothes I have! Here's what you do. Call the people in Brazil. Tell them I'm having problems with my manager, and my equipment has been locked up, but I still want to honour the contract. Give them the specifications and tell them to hire all the equipment we need, and take the cost out of whatever I'm making.' I rang the band and told them and, in the end, everybody went, Paul, City Life and Simon Said.

However, Jay got hold of the girls and, when we got to Brazil, they weren't speaking to me. They were convinced that I was against them. He had told them that I had never wanted them to work with me, and had said they had to be always back near the band, not at the front with me, and should always wear dark clothing and never be well-lit. All of this was totally untrue. When I first knew they were going to work with me I had said to Jay that the girls were used to working by themselves, they were an act on their own, they were used to performing and holding the show with no-one on the stage but them. To just be in the background wouldn't be acceptable to them. I was excited and glad to have them, because they were very good, but I thought they should open the show with some of their own numbers, ending with their own hit song (they had made an excellent recording of a disco version of the song 'Smile', with Sondra singing the lead). Jay had told them the opposite.

I suspect that Sondra, his girlfriend, talked Jay into letting them go with me, but he probably said, 'Well, you go, but you just stay away from her.' So for days they didn't speak to me, and I could hear them talking to one another about me, saying spiteful things. So it was not a happy time.

It was my birthday while we were in Brazil, so all this must have happened in late August or early in September. I was lonely, and because I knew how persuasive Jay could be, I couldn't completely blame them for believing him. They didn't know him as well as I did. Secondly, I didn't want the promoters and record company to know that we weren't getting along. So I sent the girls a letter saying that if I had done anything wrong, I hadn't intended to, and that I at least deserved an opportunity to defend myself.

Sondra was always the leader, and she told them that they should talk to me, so we got together and talked everything over, and found out that Jay had told us all a bunch of lies. We had a great birthday celebration, but sadly, and even though I was in love with their brother, we were still never quite as happy with each other again.

For years to come, not long after this trip, we split up. Because of Jay's hatred and jealousy for Linwood, he wanted to see us fail, so for his last act as my manager after the success of 'Never Can Say

---

Goodbye' he put together for me what was called 'The World's Largest Disco' at Madison Square Garden. It cost me $50,000 to put the show together but, because it was too big to take anywhere else, after all the costs were taken into account it only earned me $4,000 which put me in a very, very deep hole. Jay had squandered all my money and left much unpaid.

I think Jay's way of operating was always 'divide and conquer'. He had spent his adult life feeling, 'If I don't get them first, they're going to get me.' Nobody liked him. He'd go to the record company and raise Cain, screaming and yelling obscenities at everybody. He'd do the same thing with the agencies. I imagine he's still the same way. When we were young, we admired him. But as I got to know him better, I realized that it wasn't clever to be thrown out of every restaurant in New York. He was so belligerent and nasty.

Jay helped me get started but, if it wasn't for Linwood, I would not be singing now. I've no doubt in my mind, that if I'd had to go it alone after that fight with Jay, I would have just done what Linwood's sisters did and tried to find somebody to marry. Simon Said went on singing for a year or eighteen months although not with me. Then they left Jay, because they found him out, like I did, and soon after that they just stopped singing altogether. It is a pity, because they were excellent. Apart from their own record, 'Smile', with Sondra singing the lead, they backed me up on my recording of 'I've Got You Under My Skin', which I think is great also!

In the end, in late 1977, after a lot of really nasty legal wrangling, Polydor grew tired of the fight, and they just paid Jay off. I signed a new management contract, and began to work with Linwood.

I recorded *Glorious*, my fourth album. Then Linwood moved into offices on Park Avenue, and because all the tracks were conceived there, in 1978 we called the next album *Park Avenue Sounds*, including an excellent arrangement of 'After the Loving'. It was produced by Norman Harris, Ron Ryson and Alan Felder, and once again, it made the top 40.

Jay helped me to get started by introducing me to Paul Leka, who helped to get me my first recording contract with Columbia records. I've prayed for Jay, and I still pray for him, because once upon a time, I admired and loved him like a brother.

15

SEARCHING

As a child, the only thing I remember liking about going to church was the music, because the church that my grandmother went to had a very good youth choir. Nevertheless, something more must have seeped in somehow, because I seem to have always had a very strong faith in God – God, not Jesus. Even though the services I attended with my grandmother were almost always at Christmas and Easter, for some reason I never got hold of any idea about Jesus or thought anything about him. But even as a very small child, I used to talk to God, and every night I would say my prayers.

I can remember when I was a teenager reading an article in the *Inquirer* newspaper – which was just as popular then as it is now – about the earth and the moon which at some date – I think it was one 16 February – were going to collide. The moon was going to come and crash into the earth. Although I did not want to believe it, it seemed to me that the moon, every night after that, was getting bigger and bigger. I tried to put it out of my mind, but then I woke up in the middle of the night. I went to the bathroom, and on the way I looked out of the kitchen window and I saw this great, dense fog. The fog was very thick and a very peculiar red colour. I realized that the fog was so thick and red that I could not see the ground – and we only lived on the fourth floor. I could not even see the window of the next door neighbour, which was only inches away from ours. Suddenly I remembered that this was the date that the *Inquirer* had predicted the moon would collide with the earth.

It was the middle of the night, or very early in the morning. I believe it was a Saturday, so we were all sleeping late. As I started back to the bed, I heard a terrible noise. This was the loudest noise that I ever heard in all the days of my life. It was just indescribable. I thought, 'Yep. It's happening.'

I believed for sure that any moment now our building was going to crumble down around us, and we were all going to be crushed to death. I thought for a second of going to wake up my mother and my brothers and sister to warn them. But then I thought, 'No, why should I wake them up, if we're all going to die? Let them at least die in their sleep.'

I scurried back to bed and lay down, and I remember saying to myself a prayer:

'Dear God, please give me peace and quick sleep. And when I fall asleep and this building crumbles round us, please take us all to heaven to be with you.'

And I fell asleep – quite confident that that would happen, because of my strong faith in God.

Of course, when I woke in the morning, the sun was shining, the fog was gone, and I had no explanation for the terrible sights and sounds I'd heard in the night. The radio weather report talked about the fog, and how thick it had been; and I learned later in the day that the redness had been caused by the fact that the manager of the bar across the street from our house had forgotten to turn out his neon sign over the door the night before! The terrible noise I had heard was the first jet ever to take off from the New Newark International Airport!

I have prayed every night for as long as I can remember, for all of my family and friends and as a child I had a list that I said in the same order every night – God bless this one, God bless that one, from time to time naming some specific thing. One would need to be healed of some ailment, one needed to be given money for some bill – whatever. I would tell God and ask him to put them right.

That was about the extent of my relationship with God, until the day my mother died. I would give him my nightly grocery list, and in exchange I tried to be a good and moral person. There was nothing more to it than that. But after my mother passed away in 1970, I became more and more aware of a great emptiness in the centre of my life. I knew I was looking for something more from life, but I didn't really know what it was.

I had this yearning to see my father again. It was strange. I had hardly seen him at all since I was a child. He had tried to keep up a relationship with me, but I didn't want to know. I'd gone to his house a couple of times, until I was about eight or nine years old – my brother Siddiq took me – but I just wasn't interested in having a relationship with him. For one thing, he was living with another woman, and I didn't want to be around her. And he had two Doberman pinschers, and I didn't want to be around them either! At that time I wasn't interested in someone who didn't live with us, wasn't part of our family, and after a while he had given up and stayed away. But now I had a strong wish to make up with him, and have at least one loving parent in the world.

I also had a growing interest and desire to learn more about religion, to find somewhere I could belong in some kind of church, although not necessarily a Christian church. My feeling of wanting to find my father I kept brushing aside for the next few years. But I embarked almost immediately on my search for a deeper, more real faith. I started reading the Bible, particularly the Psalms, and attending church occasionally. At the same time I was looking into different religions: Secular Humanism, Buddhism and Transcendental Meditation . . . I even tried Hare Krishna, and Scientology, but none of it seemed in accord with the Bible. Even though I had never been a regular churchgoer, I had somehow always believed that the Bible was real, was right.

My brother Siddiq had become a Muslim. There was a period when the Black Muslims came here and, as my pastor puts it so well, Christians appeared to men to be a bunch of wimps. Most churches have about 75 to 80 per cent women, and the men are often old. They have done all the sinning that they want to do, and are now trying rather late in the day to make their peace with the Lord and get away to heaven. So when the black men of America were feeling so downtrodden, so misunderstood, so underprivileged, Christianity didn't interest them at all. But this new form of Islam, the Black Muslims, gave them a sense of pride, a sense of self-worth, a sense of respect, and a God that seemed to care about them. And they all went for it.

Siddiq was hanging on to this when he went through some terrible times in his life. He disseminated it to Arthur, my younger brother. And because Arthur admired him so much – we all did – he became a Muslim too, and has stuck with it.

I, too, looked into Islam, but I never really agreed with it, partly because of the way they treated women. Also, I just could not accept their image of God. Unlike the men, I wasn't looking for strength, or something to boost my pride and ego. I was searching for love and truth. For them a true picture of God is kind of incidental, I guess, but for me it was everything.

My feeling is that a lot of people aren't really looking for truth, or to recognize that they are made in the image of God. They are looking for a God that they can make in their own image, one who is going to be there to give them everything they want.

The rest of my family have all been on their own search for faith. I should say Ronald carries a Bible in his pocket, and claims Christ. Larry and his wife go to church nearly every Sunday. Ralph sings in his church choir, and does solos. Siddiq goes to the mosque, and Arthur – I don't know how often he goes to the mosque, I don't think he goes very much – but he reads the Koran; and Irma – Irma is sort of running from the Lord at the moment.

❖

By 1977 I didn't want to put off finding my father any longer. I decided that I must see him and, with Linwood's encouragement, I went and found him. He was living with his sister, Aunt Hilda. They were both very glad to see me, very welcoming, and we formed a really loving relationship. He became really close to Linwood, too, and because I was travelling so much Linwood saw even more of him than I did.

He was very charming, gentle, and so intelligent, and I really, really was so sorry that I'd missed all those years. This time I could say I loved him.

He only lived for another two years, and his death really grieved me. He had a beautiful funeral, organized by his sister. The minister, the Rev. Thomas that preached at his funeral was pastor of a Baptist church, and his sons are members of a group called the Crown Heights Affair which became very popular here. What a lovely man! I'll never forget that a few people came in after the service had started, and he said, 'You're late! But you've got an appointment that you're not going to be late for!' A few months later I asked him to come and perform another ceremony for me ...

It was not a grievous funeral – it was a home-going. They celebrated his salvation, his going home to be with the Lord, and they grieved only for the time that they would not be with him. And there were so many women there! They were comforting each other – there must have been six of them – it was really amazing.

I shall always regret not having spent more time with him.

My family doesn't seem to live very long – but Linwood's family live for ever. I once called his grandfather when he was ninety-three – and he couldn't come to the telephone because he was out in the yard chopping firewood.

I remember my mother telling me a story about my father being in a Liar's Club when he was young. You won a prize for telling the greatest lie. And the subject this particular time was: Who was the most afraid? Everyone was making up really scary stories about ghosts and ghouls. When it was his turn, my father told a story about how he had been caught by a farmer stealing eggs from under some chickens in a barn. And they asked him – so what was so frightening about that? And he said, 'Well, I don't know what was so frightening about it, but I do know that I was more afraid at that time than anybody else who's told about their incidents, because, when I was in the barn, and was taking the eggs out from under the chicken, the farmer poked his head in the door and looked at me and said:

'What you doin' in here, white boy?'

My father played the ukelele, guitar and sang professionally. He was the opening act for Step and Fetchit, a vaudeville comedy act. I never heard his singing voice. I've been told that my aunt has some tapes or records or something of him. He'd been with my mother to a club once to see me singing when I was about eighteen, and he told me that he had been very proud of me.

He weighed 169 pounds from the time that he was a teenager. I think he may have gained five pounds in his later years, because he had a bit of a paunch, but he was still a very slim man on the day he died. Now why couldn't I have inherited that?

He was very dark, and had thin lips, but the lower lip kind of hung down, and it was almost blue. He was not a very attractive man, physically. He just missed being ugly! You can see from his picture. Probably he was much better looking when he was younger. I do have one picture of him when he was a baby – and he was a gorgeous little baby, adorable, in a little dress!

I have a picture of Sunny and my mother when they were married, and that shows her when she was younger, and where I got my looks from. But I do look like my father, too. In fact I probably look even more like my father than I look like my mother. It is possible to look like somebody that's unattractive without being unattractive!

16

CRASH! BANG! WALLOP!

On 12 March 1978 we were working at the Beacon Theatre – my band, City Life, a male backing group of three singers and dancers, and I. I always had a pretty fast-moving stage act, involving a lot of dance routines.

We were doing a sort of apache number – I can't even remember what song it was – but one where I danced away from the background singers, and then I turned round, twisted my microphone upside down and snapped the cable like a whip, making it go back to them. They grabbed it and we would have a sort of tug of war.

Well this time they grabbed the cable, but they didn't hold it, and I fell. I fell and crashed backwards over a monitor.

We were taping the show, and Linwood was in the control room watching the screens. The camera was focused on the stage, and they could see the band, see me, and see the guys. They saw me sling the cable, and them grab for it and back up, but when I fell, I was out of the camera frame, and they couldn't see me. And from the expressions on the faces of the band members and the dancers, nobody in the control room knew that anything was in the least bit the matter. The people on stage didn't look over at me, or look in any way concerned. They didn't reach out for me. Nothing. The audience stood up. The whole audience tried to catch me. But these people didn't.

I knew that nobody had tried to catch me or come and get me, but I didn't know that they had been so uncaring, until I looked at the tape later. My thought when I saw it was, if you're walking down a street and you see a woman on the other side of the street falling, instinct makes you try to grab her. They never moved. I'd only worked with these three guys for a few months, but I thought we'd got really close. City Life – Billy, Tony, Clay and Sal – I'd worked with them for years!

Well, I rolled over, and jumped up and got back into the frame and continued dancing, and nobody knew anything about it.

A few days later I woke up in my apartment and I couldn't move. I couldn't turn over or move anything except for my arms. I reached for the telephone, called Linwood and said, 'I can't move.'

'What do you mean, you can't move?'

'I *can't move.*'

He says that by the time he got there – because he had a key to my apartment – I was screaming at the top of my voice with pain. I don't remember it. He called an ambulance and they came and got me. The next thing I remember was I was high – because they'd given me valium shots – and hungry!

I said, 'Did they get me here in time for lunch?'

I stayed in the hospital for two weeks, in traction. I felt better and they sent me home. Then two weeks later the pain came back, and I was once again in screaming agony. I went back into hospital on 15 April, and was there until 3 July.

While I was in hospital I began to read the Bible far more carefully. I was only in a semi-private room so there was always one other person with me. The woman that stayed the longest, and was the last one with me, was so impressed by my reading the Bible that she found my number later and told me she'd gone back to church because of my example. Actually, I think I was still partly doing it for show – but at least I did her some good!

And I did leave the hospital with a renewed faith in God. I was so grateful for my recovery. I felt perhaps I had been allowed to survive for some purpose. I still didn't know anything about Christ, but I felt stronger in my faith in God. I felt I wanted to encourage people. I wanted to be a better person. I wanted to be

Left: My grandmother, Fanny Smart

Below right: My mother, Queenie May

Below left: My father, Daniel Fowles

Above left: My oldest
brother, Ronald,
in 1965

Above right: My
brother, Larry

Right: Aged five
with my youngest
brother, Arthur

Left: Arthur in 1977

Below: Larry and Robert (Siddiq) in 1965

Bottom left: My little sister, Irma, in 1951

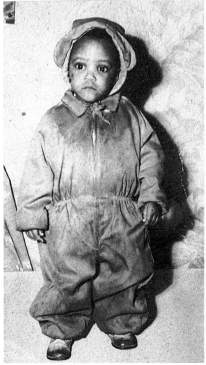

Right: With The Soul Satisfiers in 1963

Below: The Cleave Nickerson Organ Combo in 1967. Cleave could smell a Howard Johnson's restaurant from miles away!

Bottom right: City Life, featuring Gigi in 1972. I was about to sign a record contract and have my first hit

Bottom left: Tera, Sondra and Cynthia of Simon Said in 1975. Sondra, my sister-in-law, is one of my closest friends.

Top left: With David Soul in 1977

Top right: On stage in Venezuela in 1979

Right: Crowned as Disco Queen in 1979, with Linwood.

Above: With Princess Grace of Monaco at the last of her Red Cross balls in 1981

Top: With Regine and Michael Caine in 1982.

Above: The Lebanon in 1983. This was my first time in a war-zone

Right: With Engelbert Humperdinck in 1986

Above: With Malcolm Feld in 1986. Tony Blackburn is in the background

Left: With Cliff Richard following the BBC Christmas Concert in 1993

Below: With Donna Summer in 1994 – the 'Queens of Disco' together!

Above: Linwood and I with David Granoff,
Yvette Gonzalez and Jean-Paul Gaultier

Right: With Linwood and our Russian friend
Heiko in Red Square, 1994.
I performed at a benefit concert for the
children of Chernobyl.

Below: My favourite publicity shot!

more helpful. I wanted to be more like my mother had raised me.

The day I came out of hospital I was wearing a back brace and was supposed to go straight home to bed, but it was the last day of the International Disco Convention in New York. So I went home and changed and then Linwood escorted me over in a limousine with my wheelchair in the boot. They brought me in at the back of the stage in my wheelchair and set me on the dais.

Donna Summer had had several hits that year, and when she came in they gave her a standing ovation. She thanked them for the applause and said, 'But before I go on, I must recognize one person who should be home this evening, because she's just been released today from hospital after having had spine surgery, but she decided that she just could not *not* be here . . . Ladies and Gentlemen could we please have a round of applause for the First Lady of Disco – Gloria Gaynor.' And then *I* got a standing ovation. I thought that was so sweet. It really touched me. Because by then they were calling *her* Queen of Disco, but she was saying OK, I'm Queen this year, but this is still the First Lady; and you're a very classy lady, I thought.

When I came out of hospital I moved in with Linwood because, after not working for so long, I couldn't really afford to keep on my own apartment. Linwood had spent a lot of money on my health care because my hospitalization insurance didn't cover everything and, although he had kept on my apartment for me, it was becoming a financial drain and we didn't know when I'd be able to start earning again. City Life had had to carry on on their own. They didn't get another singer, and gradually broke up altogether, going off one at a time to join other people.

Linwood had just acquired a new condominium and it is where we live to this day. It's absolutely wonderful, on the fourth floor of a big apartment block on a hillside that slopes down to the Hudson River. It's quite rural round about us – many of the houses are made of timber and have big gardens. Down by the river there are some building sites and a few restaurants, but also fields of wheat and grass. And on the other side of the river is Manhattan. At night when it's all lit up, it's spectacular. When people ask me why we live in New Jersey instead of Manhattan I say, 'Because who wants to look out of their apartment at a view of New Jersey?' Besides, purchase taxes are only 6½% in New Jersey!

I came out of hospital on 3 July. I'll never forget it, because the next day was the Fourth of July, American Independence Day. We stood on Linwood's terrace and watched the Manhattan fireworks display across the Hudson River.

17

'I WILL SURVIVE'

Once I was on my feet again, after the operation, we began preparations to do another single. It was a song called 'Substitute', because the new President of Polydor New York, Freddy Hayan, had just had a big hit with it in Britain, where he had come from, with a group called Clout. He wanted to do the same thing in the United States, and chose me to do it. In the meantime, Linwood had heard about and listened to recordings by the music producer Freddy Perren. So he asked Polydor if they thought it would be a good idea to use Freddy Perren as producer for the new single, which would then be featured on the new album. They agreed.

Freddy Perren agreed to be involved if he could have the B side of the single for one of his own writer's songs. The writer, Dino Fekaris, talked to me, and we discussed the kind of things I liked to sing and the kind of subject matter I liked to deal with, and he wrote 'I Will Survive' for me – for the B side!

Dino Fekaris came along to the studio, but he'd forgotten to bring the song with him. So he just tore a brown paper bag open and wrote the lyrics on that. As we read it, Linwood and I looked at each other and said, 'You're going to put this on the B side of *what*? How could you put this on the B side? This has to be a hit.' We knew it as soon as we read the lyrics, without even hearing the haunting melody, that everybody could relate to this song.

The record company felt differently and, on its first release, 'I Will Survive' was put on the B side of 'Substitute'. No-one at Polydor wanted to buck Freddy Hayan, the new President. 'Substitute' was his baby.

91

Linwood said, 'Well, what they do doesn't matter. Because when you do live performances, we'll put this song at the end of the show and see what the people think about it. We'll let the public decide.' Ron Kreidman our lawyer has been with us for seventeen years as counsellor and trusted friend. Linwood confered with him regarding our plans. Then with Ron's support and encouragement they met Dickie Kline and Rick Stevens, heads of Polydor's A&R department. They convinced them that Rick should take 'Survive' to Ritchie, the very influential DJ of New York's world famous disco, Studio 54. Ritchie loved it, and played 'I Will Survive' often.

We went on a tour in Mexico at this time and Linwood got the DJs to play the flip side, instead of 'Substitute'. Every time I sang, or the DJs played 'I Will Survive' the response was tremendous. Other DJs began to play it in the clubs and on the radio. Finally, in 1979, Polydor published the song as the hit side. It was a number one in five different countries at one time, including the United States, Britain and South America, and over the years it has reached number one in every country that I've ever heard of at some point.

Next we produced the album *Love Tracks*, featuring 'I Will Survive', which went gold; it was my own, and the disco era's, biggest ever dance hit. It sold fourteen million copies in the first few months, and the following year I was awarded a Grammy Award for Best Disco Record.

Receiving a Grammy is one of the most coveted honours to be bestowed upon a singer in America, and I'm very honoured to have been given one, as well as to have been nominated for four others. My memories of Grammy Award ceremonies bring back feelings of both ecstasy and agony! One year I had the honour, along with Isaac Hayes, to present the Grammy for the Best Male Group.

At the rehearsal the night before the show I met up with Isaac and we agreed that we didn't want to look stupid and mechanical as one can if you read everything off the cue cards, so we took the time to memorize all the cards we had to read.

On the night I couldn't decide whether to wear a sequined gown or a gold lamé cocoon dress that I had bought for the presentation. I decided on the gold lamé, a glamorous affair with a fishtail bottom that I'd had designed for me by the LA designer Eileen

Warren. I looked fabulous – at least, Linwood and I thought so! I was doubly pleased when I got there and saw that nearly all the other ladies were wearing sequins. I felt like the belle of the ball!

Isaac and I waited backstage until it was time for us to make our presentation. Then someone told us: 'When you get out, pass the first podium, and go to the second, and make the presentation from there.'

Simple enough, right? Sure. Except that I didn't realize that from where I was standing, I couldn't see the first podium. So as we walked across the stage, I was about to walk straight past the *second* podium, totally confident that there was another podium ahead, and thinking how great I must be looking on camera! Isaac, gentleman that he is, gently steered me back towards the correct podium. I hadn't had stage fright since High School, but now I began to feel the first twinges of nervousness as I realized that I had been about to make such a mistake.

We stood together at the podium, and we used the cue cards only for timing, remembering every line and who was to say what. And we were doing great, until Isaac said: 'And the winner is . . . The Bee Gees!' and at that point a cue card came up that I had never seen before – the one that's apparently always used when the winner, or winners, aren't at the ceremony. So I read:

'Ladies and Gentlemen. The Bee Gees are not here, but we congratulate . . . him, her or them . . .' Aghh! I could not stop the words from coming out of my mouth, and when they did it seemed to me that they hung on the air for at least half an hour, while I stood there with a death-grip on the podium, half wanting to cry, and half wanting to laugh, feeling completely humiliated. I looked over at Linwood in the audience and saw him trying to disappear under his seat. I finally said in a shaky voice that betrayed all I was feeling: 'Isaac! I *told* you I didn't want to read!'

Isaac put one arm around me and with the other prised my fingers loose from the podium and waving at the camera he said, 'Thank you' and through clenched teeth said to me, 'We're going to walk off to the left now.' I managed what I hoped was a reasonably sane smile at the audience and in two more seconds it was over. Phew!

When I sang 'I Will Survive' I was relating it to my recovery from spine surgery. And because the word was going round after my accident that 'the Queen of Disco is dead', one of my main thoughts was that my career would survive! And in a funny way it was also, for me, to do with surviving the death of my mother. I know for most people the song is about abusive relationships and women asserting their independence of men and all that sort of thing and of course I have suffered in that way myself, but for some reason, I was never thinking of that when I sang it.

It's been wonderful, because so many people have come to me with things they have survived. I've had children tell me that they thought they were not going to pass their exams, a man who was encouraged to go on living after one failed attempt at suicide, a woman who had felt drawn to my concert before going home where she had intended to do away with herself and 'Survive' encouraged her to abandon the idea: in all kinds of ways people have told me this song has been an encouragement to them. I think it's just one of those songs, rather like 'Bridge Over Troubled Water' by Simon and Garfunkel, that has captured the universal imagination. So I'm really, really blessed that I've been able to do that, and to have this song. But although I have always been able to sing the words with great conviction, it has still taken me a long, long time to really learn its lesson for myself.

Early in 1979, I was in the apartment one day, and Linwood called me from the office. I was asleep. He said, 'Let's get married.' I said, 'Huh?' and he said, 'Let's get married' and I said, 'OK' and I hung up. I lay back down. And then I woke up. I dialled him back at the office and said, 'Did you just call me?'

He said, 'Yeah.'

I said, 'Did you just ask me to marry you?'

He said, 'Yeah.'

'Did I say "OK"?'

'Yeah.'

So I said, 'OK' and hung up again.

I asked him, later, whether he had asked to marry me because certain people had questioned our relationship. And I asked him why he had waited to marry me. I wondered if he hadn't wanted to marry me while it seemed that I was the one that was making all the money. Now by this time he had his own offices on Park Avenue, he'd been offered membership of the Chamber of Commerce, he'd been offered membership of the National Association of Artists' Managers, he had established his own publishing company, he'd had a few songs released and he had his own income, independent of me and what he earned from being my manager. So I thought that that was what he had been waiting for, to marry me.

Somehow he thought I was asking him if he was only marrying me to show the people in the business that it wasn't just for my money.

That's not what I meant at all, and even if I thought that, I would never have said it. But I didn't think that. I was at last feeling a little bit of security that, even with him being financially secure in his own right, he was asking me to marry him. The truth is I didn't really have any money in the first place! What little I had had, I had no access to after Jay had a judgment put on it. And I didn't have *that* much, because of the $50,000 show Jay had put together, from which I only made $4000. So Linwood was the only one who had any money all along. But now he was earning real money, money that the public could see he had.

Anyway, he got very insulted, and I've never been able to straighten it out with him, but I hope that he reads this and finally understands what I meant.

❖

So we set the date to get married, 9 October 1979, his parents' wedding anniversary, and I got in touch with the Baptist minister, Rev. Thomas who had preached so well at my father's funeral. He said he would be more than glad to do it.

The stupid thing was that, because Linwood was so nervous and I was so happy that at last we were going to marry we never thought about the things you needed to have for a wedding. I only remembered a few days before that I didn't even have a dress to wear. I had quickly to make my own wedding gown. Linwood thought it was ridiculous to have a huge wedding and spend all that money to feed a whole lot of people who couldn't care less, so we were going to have a private wedding.

Now in the back of my mind was the thought 'He's being very stingy.' I'd always wanted a big, luxurious and wonderful wedding, with lots of friends and family. But if this man was going to marry me, I was going to do it whatever way he wanted. I was not going to throw any monkey wrenches in the works.

The marriage was to take place in the living room with no-one present except his mother and father, a photographer, and the minister. But the day before the wedding, I woke up to the fact that we didn't have a marriage licence, we didn't have a blood test, and I had barely finished making my dress, which was nothing but a glorified kaftan. It was very pretty, made of cream-coloured crêpe-backed satin, with champagne lace, but here I was, still making it at five o'clock in the evening the night before we were going to be married, with no blood test and no licence. So I called the minister and told him I was sorry, but we would have to postpone it.

He said, 'Look, I don't like postponements. You chose a date to get married, and that's the day you're supposed to get married, and I think you should. This is what you have to do. Tomorrow morning, go to your doctor, tell him you need a blood test right away, tell him you need the results right away; he will send you to the lab, you will get your results; go to the place where you get your marriage licence. All you have to have is a marriage *licence*. It's between you and God what day you get married. Just because the State doesn't confirm or accept it until you can get their stamp doesn't make any difference – you're going to get married tomorrow.' And we did.

As soon as 'I Will Survive' was released in Britain, British agents seemed to be flying in by every plane to try to book me for a tour there. One English agent, Malcolm Feld, arrived and offered to put my show on at the London Palladium. I think what really clinched the deal as far as Linwood was concerned was that Malcolm offered, as part of the package, that Linwood and I would fly over on Concorde! It was a great new experience for anyone at the time. Anyway, they agreed a deal for me to go over for five days in the Palladium in April 1979. People told Malcolm that he was crazy to put Gloria Gaynor, a disco artist, in the Palladium, but he had seen my show in New York and been convinced that I was more than just disco, that this new song would hit a much wider, more middle-of-the-road market, and that if people would just come to the first night, word would get around about how good the show was and the other nights would do well.

Concorde was a great thrill. But when we arrived Malcolm Feld was a very worried man, because it had got down to just over a week before the show, and he had called the box office to ask if he could reserve fifty tickets for friends, and the guy had said, 'You can have as many tickets as you want.' There were 35,000 seats to be sold for the five nights, and only 600 had gone. But the guy also said, 'But don't worry. We haven't done the mail yet.'

Malcolm didn't know what that meant, and he did worry. For about three or four days he was ringing round everyone he knew. And then, about two days before the first show, he called to get 250 tickets, and the guy said, 'You can't even have the fifty you asked for.' The entire show was sold out for five nights and we had to do a sixth night.

The Palladium had been short-staffed through illness, and when they said, 'We haven't done the mail yet,' they meant they hadn't opened the six or seven *sacks* of mail from people who had written in for tickets and enclosed cheques!

Malcolm got a call from Pinewood Studios saying that Farah Fawcett Majors and her husband, Lee Majors, who were over making a film, very much wanted to come to the show. They hadn't been able to get tickets, and could he let them have a couple. The only way he could do that was by persuading Louis Benjamin, the manager of the Palladium, to let them have the Royal Box. That same day Polydor had telephoned Malcolm to say I had got a gold disc for 'I Will Survive', and they wanted the presentation to be made on stage at the Palladium. Malcolm Feld went to the Royal Box to say hello to Farah Fawcett Majors and her husband. She thanked him for arranging it for them, and on the spur of the moment Malcolm asked her if she would do him a favour. Would she come up on stage and make the presentation of the gold disc? She gently pointed out that she was wearing a T-shirt and jeans, and Lee Majors was in jeans and a leather jacket, and they really weren't dressed to appear on the stage, so Malcolm backed off feeling embarrassed that he'd even asked her. He said afterwards that he hadn't seen past her beautiful face and hair!

Anyway, someone from the record company made the presentation, and I gave a little curtain speech, thanking everybody. I thanked Malcolm for having me at the Palladium, and I thanked the record company and the producers and all that, and then I looked and saw Linwood at the side of the stage, and so I thanked him. I asked him to come out onto the stage so the people could see him, because we had not long ago become engaged to be married.

He rather sheepishly and shyly walked out onto the centre stage and I took his hand until he seemed more confident. And I was still talking to the audience about him and how he'd been so instrumental in my career and all that when I heard the band strike up behind me. I turned round and Linwood was doing this dance called the Rock, which is a very sexy sort of dance where you bend your knees and swing your knees and your hands from side to side. The audience gave him a standing ovation, and I was saying, 'This man's too much! He's here for two seconds, and he's stolen my show! Get off my stage!' And he'd been so timid about coming out there! But he finally danced himself off the stage.

I've always been very kindly treated by the press, but I had one bad notice after one of the Palladium shows. The reporter ended his review by saying 'Gloria Gaynor moved across the stage like a wounded buffalo.' I think he must have been a rock fan! I mean, with a sold-out show at the Palladium for six nights, how bad could I have been? To say nothing of the fact that I was wearing a British size 12 and was looking quite shapely!

❖

'I Will Survive' is still in great demand even today, and it is the number one karaoke selection. Not that that does me much good! It has never stopped selling and being played. People just won't forget it. I rerecorded it in Italy in 1990, on an album called *Gloria Gaynor '90* which went gold in 1991. It was re-released in Britain in 1994 and made number five in the charts, bringing me to 'Top of the Pops' twice in a week. It has been remixed and rereleased I don't know how many times in European and South American countries. But in the United States it has never been rerecorded or rereleased, until now. Radikal records have just produced a new album, and this is the first time 'I Will Survive' will have been rereleased in the United States since 1979.

As I write, it is once more number one in the Australian charts, having been released with songs from the soundtrack of the movie *Priscilla, Queen of the Desert* with Terence Stamp and also has just been released in the US and several European countries on a 'Gloria Gaynor's Greatest Hits' album.

As for me – I've travelled round the world with it!

18

THE WORLD IS OUR OYSTER

I have travelled all over the world, to more than 75 countries, and stayed in places of awesome beauty in Australia, New Zealand, Japan, Singapore, Indonesia, the Philippines, the Middle East, South America, some of the Eastern bloc countries, every single country in Western Europe ... England is probably my favourite country to visit, mainly because I have so many dear friends there, but we've made good friends and learned something about different cultures and customs in all of the countries we've visited. It has helped us to grow and develop a much broader outlook on life. In a strange way, travelling helps you to understand that life is very short, and that we should be living each day to the fullest extent possible.

In Britain I've been honoured to sing for a big charity event held at Buckingham Palace, organized by Anne Shelton; I've sung before the Duke of Edinburgh; we were invited over to a big party at the Hilton Hotel on the eve of the wedding of Prince Charles and Princess Diana, and I remember that particularly well, because our host gave me a £100 raffle ticket, and I won a fur coat! Over the years I've done hundreds of tours and shows all over Britain and appeared on television dozens of times.

Of all the countries I've visited, I think Italy likes *me* best. I've been to more places in Italy than the average Italian, and I've been going back every year since 1975. I've seen their beautiful Alps, their lush green valleys, their blue-green sea coast with superb beaches, the marinas, the art galleries, the churches, the architecture and the food. I've had too much great pasta, *calamari fritti* (which is fried squid), *zucchini fritti* (fried squash), too much risotto, and far, far too much rich chocolate dessert! I was a slim and lovely girl when I first visited Italy!

On one of our first visits to Italy, Linwood and I took along a friend, Norma Jenkins, from New Jersey, who was also a singer. Norma had never travelled internationally and we thought we'd give her the experience of performing before a foreign audience. Norma is far more flamboyant than I could ever be, and whenever we entered a hotel or restaurant, they always thought that she was the star! I must admit that it irritated me rather, but I guess she did look and behave more like people expect stars to be.

One day we were in a supermarket, and we had separated to shop. A woman came over to me and speaking in English but with a heavy Italian accent, she said, pointing to Norma, 'Ees that Glowria Gaynor?'

I said, 'No. No, it isn't.'

She said, 'It's OK, you canna tella me. I'mma no bother her. It's a Glowria Gaynor, no?'

I said, 'No, I assure you, it isn't.' This woman wouldn't have it! She approached Norma, and I mouthed to her over the woman's shoulder, 'Don't you dare!' Norma darted round the corner of the next aisle and met me at the door, and we left laughing.

Another time on tour in Italy, the band and I were travelling on a luxury tour bus through the night. I had fallen asleep lying on the long seat at the back of the bus, when something caused me to wake up. I sat up and looked out of the front window, and I could see that we had stopped in front of an overpass. The driver seemed to be sizing it up. I lay down again, and then jumped up again as I felt the bus go racing forward, and then jerk to a halt. He'd charged, and jammed the bus under the overpass. The skylight shattered and glass was showering everywhere, all over the startled band members, who were violently awoken from their sleep. I warned them not to cut themselves, trying to get glass out of their hair, but to wait until we got to our hotel and could use a vacuum cleaner!

It was two in the morning, and there we were, with all our luggage, standing waiting on the highway for another bus, which came in about an hour and a half. We reloaded, and went off again. A couple of hours later, I woke up again, and couldn't see anything out of any of the windows. The driver appeared to be hunched over the wheel as though he couldn't see where he was going, and we were creeping along very slowly. Suddenly the bus hit something that jolted the entire bus and nearly knocked us all out of our seats. There was a very, very strange noise outside the bus. As the bus doors opened, we realized that it was being made by hundreds of chickens, and we were in the middle of them. The driver had mistaken an alley for a narrow street, and had driven the bus straight into someone's barn. Could all this possibly have happened in one night? We couldn't believe it. Ah! the glamorous life of us international singing stars!

In 1982 we went to Egypt, a long-looked-forward-to trip. I performed at the Mina House from where we could see the great pyramid of Cheops, at 452 feet the highest pyramid of Egypt. President Sadat's daughter was in the audience that night. After the show we climbed up inside the pyramid and marvelled at how huge the stones were. We wondered how they could possibly have engineered and built it. And nearby was the Sphinx, 189 feet long and absolutely amazing.

We were taken to a party where we enjoyed a show of dancing horses. We also visited a school where children are taught to weave carpets from the age of five. These children create pictures in their minds and weave them into the carpet as they go along, one strand of yarn at a time, across the loom. It's magical.

They said if you drink from the Nile you will be sure to return – but it was so dirty, I only pretended. We rode horses while we were there and, one day while we were out walking, we came across a man with a camel with what looked like an offering plate in front of him. George Braxton, our drummer, asked how much it would cost to get on the camel. The man said, 'Nothing.'

George said, 'Really? Can I get on?'

The man said, 'Sure.' The camel knelt down, and George got on. When the camel stood up, the man said, 'But it costs $5 to get off!'

I love visiting Spain, because I can speak the language. In all

Spanish-speaking countries I always sing 'I Will Survive' in Spanish, and I've also recorded it in Spanish.

Whenever we visit a new country, I make it my business to learn at least a few simple phrases in the native language. After all, apart from in Spain, I sing the entire concert in English, so I think it's nice if I can speak to the audience a little bit in their own language.

So when I went to Beirut in 1983, I found a language teacher who taught me ten words and phrases in Arabic – all of which I've since forgotten except 'Ma'haba' which means 'Hello', 'Shukran' which means 'Thank you', 'Anabadaish' which means 'I will survive', and 'Ana bahebak ya Libnon' which means 'I love you, Lebanon.' The teacher said I pronounced them with hardly any accent, and we were thrilled.

We landed in Lebanon and were taken to the hotel in Beirut. On the way, we passed through several roadblocks put up by the different factions that were occupying the war-torn city. I was surprised to see how beautiful and modern the clothes were that people were wearing. There was obviously still much affluence there, and many of the buildings were made of a beautiful white stone. The architecture was exotic and like none I'd ever seen. There were also more familiar styles of building, big office blocks and stores like you'd see at home. The area was quite metropolitan, but marred by the holes and craters made by bombs, shells and mortars. It was my first time in a war-zone, but as we passed by, people would wave and call out, 'Welcome to our country!' so it all seemed very warm and friendly.

The next day we were taken on a tour of the city. Soldiers from the Israeli army, the Lebanese and the Syrians, all escorted us together. They laughed and talked with us, and with each other, so we felt quite well protected, although it was a bit worrying when one of them would suddenly shoot off one of those guns from their hips. Many of the soldiers were just teenagers.

We were at the UN the day before it was bombed. We went to a US army camp and visited the men on patrol the day before the infamous car bombing. We saw fox-holes and how the soldiers live during war-time, and with every step I thanked God that I couldn't be drafted! I had had no idea what to expect, so I was wearing very feminine white sandals that got all muddy and a white sleeveless dress in soft fabric. I nearly froze. Would you have known it was freezing cold in the desert?

I was performing for the soldiers that night, and couldn't wait to change into a warmer outfit, and to be dancing under the hot lights. God bless the men of the armed forces who go out and have to endure so much to protect our countries.

The next evening I was performing for the general public. Once again as we drove through the city we passed lots of roadblocks. There was an excited crowd waiting to greet me. The applause and cheers were deafening as I ascended a wooden stage that had been assembled in the middle of a football field. They only died down when the musical introductions began. As soon as the crowd recognized each song, they cheerfully sang along with me in broken phonetic English and, as I finished each song and ventured one of my words in Arabic, they seemed thrilled beyond measure, and called my words back to me in Arabic. 'Thank you! Hello! How are you?' The response of the crowd had risen to fever pitch, and at last, at the end of the programme, when I spoke the Arabic word 'Anabadaish' meaning 'I Will Survive' the cheers were deafening, and they all repeated 'Anabadaish! Anabadaish!'

The instruments began to play the introduction to the song, and I had saved my best until last: I was going to give them the one long phrase I'd mastered in Arabic. I shouted out to them in the best Arabic I could 'Ana bahebak ya Libnon!' I love you Lebanon.

A dead silence fell over the crowd. I thought, 'I know I got it right.' Perhaps they haven't understood me. I shouted out again, 'Ana bahebak ya Libnon!' Still – dead silence. By this time the instrumental introduction to 'I Will Survive' was nearly ended, so I thought I'd better stick to what I knew, singing. So I just shouted out one more time, 'Anabadaish!', 'I will survive!' and they all shouted back 'Anabadaish!' to my great relief. I sang 'I Will Survive', and bowed and left the stage with the audience clamouring for an encore. As I started to return to the stage, Linwood grabbed my arm and hissed in my ear, 'Forget the linguistics – just sing!'

'Why? What did I do wrong?'

'You were saying "I love you, Lebanon!" '

'I know. What's wrong with that?'

'We're in Syria!'

I mean, we'd been showing our passports every ten minutes to someone. How was I to know that, within a couple of hours' drive from the hotel, one of those hundreds of roadblocks was actually a border that let us into Syria, where they *don't* love Lebanon? Fortunately, even though I'd told them I loved Lebanon, the Syrians still loved me!

We've been to several Eastern bloc countries. We went to Warsaw and Gdansk in Poland during the time of Solidarity demonstrations in 1982. I did a TV show in Gdansk but, although there was a large audience, they seemed tense and unresponsive. The TV cameras had a hard time keeping up with me as I reinforced their likely opinion that Americans are wild and unruly by jumping off the stage and going through the audience, encouraging them to clap and sing along. They loosened up and began to have a good time, although there were people watching who did not approve. Later that night, Linwood and I were refused entrance to our hotel discotheque. They said it was closed but we could hear the music and could see people dancing. We certainly must have offended someone.

More recently, in Kazakhstan, we have learned something of the hardships of the lives of people living in Eastern European countries since the break-up of the Soviet Union. We saw some great contrasts. We were well received by our hosts but they had very little. The meals did not begin to measure up to the luxury that we take for granted even in a fast food restaurant. Yet we knew they were giving us the most and the best that was available, and that they themselves could never afford to eat like they were feeding us. We tried to buy things, but no-one would take the local currency we had changed our dollars for; they all just wanted dollars. Not that there was much to buy. The shelves in almost all the shops and stores were empty. The whole place looked as though it had been abandoned for some years, and when the people came back they hadn't bothered to repair or fix up anything. We were told that, when they got rid of the oppressive government that had been taking care of them, and now that democracy had been restored, no-one wanted to work unless they could make a lot of money. Nobody wanted to do the menial jobs of cleaning and repairing the infrastructure, so none of it was being done. The average salary was about £100 a month.

By contrast to all this poverty, our show was held in a huge amphitheatre built into a mountainside, with state-of-the-art lights, stage equipment, television cameras, and a VIP section with a television monitor for each table. The event was an international talent contest, with judges flown in from all over Europe and the United States. The contestants were all aspiring artists and I was the professional 'guest star' for the evening. Of course all of this was being paid for by the government.

After the performance we had a sumptuous meal, complete with caviar and champagne, hosted by the mayor of the city, and attended only by the international judges and promoters and Linwood and me. Linwood had spent all afternoon with our agent Heiko Gunther, and the promoters who had brought us to the event, and they all had been talked into trying some Russian vodka. By the time we went in to dinner, they were beginning to feel it. As we entered the dining hall, which was nicely decorated, with flowers all along the six long tables, we were introduced to the mayor, who looked like a cross between a Samurai warrior and a Sumo wrestler, and the other judges.

Thanks to a combination of the effects of the vodka and the high altitude, Linwood was being an even more than usually animated version of his always outgoing self. He was introducing himself to all the people as they came into the dining room. Suddenly the mayor, sitting at the centre of the top table, said in a loud voice to Linwood, 'You sit down!'

Linwood said, 'I know you're not talking to me. You don't talk to me like that.' He didn't recognize the mayor, but I didn't realize that, and I got really nervous. Sitting beside me was the American judge. I said to her, 'Do you know what's going on here?'

She said, 'Well, the mayor is wielding his power, and your husband has had a little too much vodka.'

The mayor stood up and said to Linwood, 'You sit down now! I am Dictator!'

Linwood said, 'Now you look, boy! I'm an American. I don't have any Dictator. I do the dictating.' I was tugging at his jacket and pleading with him to sit down. It was difficult, because Linwood was calling this man 'a clown' and getting himself all wound up. Eventually I got him to sit down.

It eventually became clear what the mayor was doing. He wanted everyone to sit so that he could call each country's representative one at a time, so they could introduce themselves to everyone else at once, and give their assessment of the evening's proceedings. The mayor spoke very little English, but he had an interpreter and the introductions went on as he had ordained. When it came to our turn, he asked me to speak. I thanked him for the invitation and congratulated him on the organization of the whole event. I said I thought it was a wonderful idea and opportunity for his country's aspiring artists to be seen. And then I sat down.

I had been the last one, and then the mayor stood up, and his interpreter relayed his speech to us, which ended with a special welcome and thanks to me for coming. He showered me with accolades for my performance. Then he said to Linwood – in English, and in the same stern tone: 'You stand up!' Linwood stood up quickly, ready for anything. The mayor took his interpreter by the hand and led her round the long table to where Linwood was standing. Through his interpreter the mayor then said to Linwood:

'Sir, if I have said or done anything to offend you this evening, please accept my apology. I, too, am an unreasonable man!' He then put his arms around Linwood's waist and lifted him from the floor. Then Linwood put his arms around the mayor's waist, but could only get him to his toes. The rest of us all sat and looked on in wonder as Linwood and the mayor became best buddies! Linwood became something of a local hero for the rest of our stay and, the next morning, when we went into the dining room for breakfast, he got a standing ovation.

Then there was Moscow where we stayed at the Savoy Hotel. It is as lavish, and as ostentatious a place as you'll find anywhere in the whole world, with glass and gilded ceilings, polished brass banisters up the great staircases, and gorgeous paintings in gilded frames lining the walls. The dining room had live performances by artists dressed in white wigs and traditional Russian costume. The food was fantastic. I had been invited there to do a benefit concert for the sick children who had been victims of Chernobyl. We attended a party given for the children who were well enough and I sang for them. Then we went to the hospital to see and sing for the others. The next morning we spent an hour taking photographs in Red Square. At Moscow airport we had meant to buy caviar, until we noticed, much to our surprise, it was more expensive there than in the United States.

Even as I'm writing this, we are preparing for another trip to Brazil. We have done lots of tours and shows and TV shows over the past twenty years in South America, and have always been warmly received by audiences everywhere, but sometimes the contrast between the life of the rich and the poor in some of these countries has brought me to tears.

In an early trip to Argentina I met Eddie Sierra, whom we later sponsored to come to the United States and become my co-writer. Eddie is a lovely man and a terrific writer. The first thing he ever did for me was put a melody to the song I'd written as a poem ten years before I met him, 'I'm Still Yours', which went on my album *Experience Gloria Gaynor*. He's also written several songs that I'm yet to record.

In Bolivia I met someone I would have loved to have as a life-long friend, but of whom my husband did not approve. His name was Catire. He was an eighteen-month-old lion! Everyone was afraid of him, except me and his trainer. I would go into his cage and play with him. I thought Linwood would pass out when Catire took my shoulder in his mouth. I just punched him in his head and said I wasn't a meatloaf! Linwood was yelling to the trainer, 'Get her out of there now, before she ends up as dinner!'

I didn't know why they were all so afraid, Catire was so cuddly and loveable. But later, in the restaurant, I had to leave because they wouldn't put their cat away. They would not believe that I have a terrible fear of cats – *little* cats!

This reminds me of the day when I was reading the Bible and I came to 1 John 4:18, which says, 'Perfect love casts out fear.' I prayed, 'Lord, if your love is perfected in me, please cast out this awful fear that I have of cats. I call it done, in the name of Jesus.' Then I just believed that it was done. A few months later, when I'd forgotten all about it, my girlfriend's son came up behind me when I was visiting them, and just as he was saying, 'Are you afraid of cats?' he dumped this huge black cat in my lap. And I felt no fear whatsoever. I had honestly and truly been delivered.

In 1988, I think it was, I was in Japan, and I had been intending to go on from there to an engagement in England, but Linwood telephoned to tell me that that was off, and so I decided to fly home to New York via Los Angeles, where one of my four best friends, Fippy, lives. Fippy's real name is Florence Dixon. I telephoned Fippy and told her I was leaving Japan on 3 July, and would like to spend the Fourth of July celebrations with her and her family in LA. She was delighted, of course, and said she'd meet me at the airport, where my plane was due to land at midday.

I left Japan on 3 July at two o'clock in the afternoon, and flew through the night, and got back to LA at one o'clock the following afternoon. When I got my luggage and everything in LA airport, Fippy was not there. I supposed she'd been held up by the children, or something, so I waited for a half hour, and she still wasn't there. I called the house, and no-one answered, so I supposed she must be on the way. I waited a bit longer, but she didn't come, and I was tired of the airport, and there was nowhere to sit, so I decided to take a taxi up to her house. I was sure somebody would be there.

No-one was. So I sat on my luggage outside to wait. Then I heard a rustling noise behind me. There was Fippy's husband, Carl, digging in the garden. I said, 'Carl! Where's Fippy?'

And he said 'G.G.!' (they call me G.G.) 'What are you doing here?'

I said, 'Well I told Fippy I was coming, and she was supposed to pick me up at the airport, is that where she went?'

'No. Fippy went to church. Some kind of meeting they're having at the church. But Fippy wasn't expecting you until tomorrow.'

'Why? I told her I'd be in on the Fourth.'

'Because tomorrow is the Fourth!'

I had left Japan on 3 July at two in the afternoon, flown through the night, and arrived in LA at one in the afternoon on the same day. It didn't seem possible, but if you cross the international date line backwards – that's what happens!

While I visited the UN in 1978, Andrew Young, the American Ambassador, named me Honorary Goodwill Ambassador for the United States. I've met many lovely people, experienced many strange cultures, seen beautiful lands and tasted wonderful new foods. Yet I am two-hundred-and-fifty-nine-and-a-half per cent American, and all these travels have left me with the certainty that God has blessed America.

19

SEWN UP

I look into the mirror some mornings these days, and it scares me. I think, 'Wow! I'm turning into my mother.' And yet, I've always wanted to be like my mother. She was a good, beautiful and talented lady.

One of her gifts was sewing, and, as I've told you, she used to make our clothes – a thing which I didn't always appreciate at the time! I never asked her to teach me. But just before she died I had bought some navy blue fabric for her to make a dress for me. It was a sort of shiny material that looks like soft leather, but it isn't leather. Mamma had measured me up, and cut it out, but she never got to sew it up. She went into hospital for the last time, and she died.

Afterwards, as I was sorting out her things, when I was looking over her sewing machine, I came across this dress, all cut out, and I thought, 'What have I got to lose?' So I tried to sew it up myself, using her machine. It came out really well! And that's how I started making my own clothes, and I've been doing it ever since.

Usually I only make clothes for wearing at home, but once in a while I'll make something for the stage.

I did a show at the end of 1994 at Studio 54, in Manhattan – on 54th Street, naturally – it was *the* Discotheque of the seventies and all of the clubs in the world tried to model themselves on Studio 54. They reopened it recently, and they had me to do the Grand Opening – I never know why the Grand Opening always comes so long after the actual opening – but they had me do it, and there was a lot of press there, and they took lots of pictures of me. One of the

111

pictures showed up again a week later in *The Star* – on the fashion page – and the title of the article was 'What They Are Wearing Now' and they had lots of superstars, and what we were wearing. Well of all the things that I should get noticed for wearing – I had made that dress! I've spent a fortune on top designer models in my life!

They thought this dress was marvellous. And there a designer there, who has a group that she calls Plus Models – they wear size fourteen and up, and she came in and said, 'Oh this dress is *divine!*' They all made such a big deal out of this thing – probably the cheapest thing that I have in my entire wardrobe!

I copy the style from a dress that was made for me in the seventies. It's a cocoon top, with what I call a 'fish-tail' bottom. The top is of fuchsia sequins, and the tail is made of fuchsia satin. As a matter of fact I wore that very dress on the 1993 Christmas programme on the BBC.

The first cocoon dress that I ever had was one that I called The Mermaid, because it was made of gold lamé, had a gold print, sort of muted and not defined print, with pinky, bluey colours mixed in. And then I bought one by a designer called Norma Carmalley, which was just a dress, but the dress came up and was so short in the front, I could never wear it, so I made a skirt to go under it. I often wore it – and I'm *still wearing it* – from the seventies! About seven years later I said to Linwood, 'I've got four cocoons, and I've really got to find something different to wear, because people are going to say: "Is that all she knows to wear?" '

So I went shopping, and I couldn't find anything that was really flattering, because I thought I was so fat – I'm fifty pounds heavier now, but then I thought I was really fat – and I could not see anything but cocoons! I thought, 'This style is never going to go out – it's become a classic!'

It's such a simple thing to make. Have you ever tried to make a paper aeroplane? That's how you make a cocoon! You fold it, like the first fold for a paper aeroplane, you sew it up, leaving room for your arms – and that's it. It's made! And if it's a soft fabric, it just lies in feminine, luxurious folds.

I tend to dress according to how I feel. I have a wide taste, and

I've never been one to dress only according to current styles. By that I mean I don't let fashion designers tell me how to dress. This year red and white are in, and that's what everybody's going to wear. Well I couldn't care less. As a matter of fact, I prefer to wear what's *not* in, because I don't want to see myself coming every time I walk down the street.

On a daily basis I dress according to how I feel. If I wake up in the morning feeling tired, I'll probably wear jeans or a jogging suit. And if I get up feeling really spry, then I'll probably wear some really smart trousers and a tank top. I wear a lot of tank tops, with an overblouse. But they'll be colourful if I'm feeling really up. They'll be bright designer colours. I *love* bright, in-your-eye, designer colours. I don't particularly care for muted colours. But I love fuchsia and aquamarine and golden yellow, or a bright canary yellow. And when I wear something like that, a bright canary yellow tank top, I'll wear it with a darker colour, that's going to kind of tone it down, so I don't look like a canary coming down the street!

My hair usually goes along with the way I feel, too. If I'm feeling a bit down, I often wear a small hat that will sort of hide me, because I don't want anybody to see me like this. I'll be sort of incognito; you wouldn't look at me and think, 'I wonder if that's Gloria Gaynor!' But if I'm feeling bright and cheery and quite pleased with myself that day – say I've got on the scales that morning and discovered I've lost a pound or two! – then I really want to be seen, and I'll wear nice jewellery that people will notice, and a hairstyle that is different. And I'll make sure that every hair is in the right place.

I've always done my own hair. My first profession after school was as a cosmetologist, and I specialized in short hairstyles and make-up. I cut everybody's hair. I told all the young people that they would look so much more mature with short hair, and I told all the older people that they would look so much younger if they got a haircut! I loved to cut hair.

I wear my own hair short when I'm in a hurry because I wear wigs. If the day has a lot of things crammed in, then I'll wear a short wig, short 'wash and wear' hair. But if I'm not in that much of a hurry, or I'm going some place where I'm concerned that people have an image of me that I don't want to shatter, then I'll try to look nice. I'll put on a really stylish outfit – it doesn't have to be designer. It just has to be something that I like how I look in. Because I think that, no matter what you are wearing, what is most impressive to people is how you feel in what you're wearing. So if you feel confident, then you'll look good. So that's the way I dress.

I used to make a lot of my own clothes. I don't so much now, because I don't get the time any more. But I do make most of my trousers because although I'm only five foot six, I wear the same length trousers as my husband, who is six feet. My legs are really very long. I wear a thirty-two-inch leg, so it's difficult for me to find trousers in the styles I like that are the right length. So I make them. It takes me two hours to make a pair of trousers.

I go into my dining room, clear off the candle-holders, spread out the fabric, cut out the pattern, and hey presto! I also make things to wear about the house, particularly kaftans. I like to be loose and really comfortable, but a bit elegant.

Linwood likes the way I dress, but he doesn't particularly like me in jeans except when I really make everything match. If I wear blue denims with a matching blue denim blouse, or a blouse with blue in it, and a blue denim cap, then it's OK, but he doesn't like it if I dress sloppily. He likes me to keep my hair done nicely, but he doesn't particularly like me in make-up. He prefers me natural.

I remember I had done a really good job – or what I *thought* was a really good job – on my make-up one night. We were going out to dinner, and we were sitting across the table looking dreamily at each other and smiling, and he said, 'You've got such beautiful eyes …' and I said, 'Thank you …' and he said, 'Well, but not with all that gook on them!' Ha! Well, thanks a lot, Bud!

So that's how I found out that he likes me to look natural. He likes the make-up that I wear during the week. I wear a bit of powder to keep down the shine. He hates it if I go out without lipstick. I think he gets that from his mother. She thinks that the moment a woman walks out of the door, she ought to have lipstick on. I wear eyeliner on the top and bottom, but very thin and close to the eyelid, so it brings out the eye but doesn't look like you are wearing make-up. He doesn't mind my wearing false eyelashes when I'm on stage, or dressing formally to go out, but they are relatively short and natural looking, so nobody ever knows.

Nobody usually knows that I'm wearing a wig either, unless I'm wearing some outlandish hairstyle. The only time I don't wear a wig is when it's really hot. When it's hot I wear a pony tail or an Afro, just natural kinky.

I remember once, years ago, I was in front of Port Authority in New York, a big bus and train station, and they have Interstate buses and trains. I had come from New Jersey into New York, and I think I was going up to Johnny Nash's. I came out of the building and a gust of wind came along and blew my wig off. Well, nobody knew it was my wig, because I was leaning against the building, laughing so hard. And my hair looked nice underneath. My hair is nice, I really like my hair, except that it's very, very soft, and if I'd come out of that building without my wig, just with my natural hairstyle, that gust of wind would have blown my hairstyle right out. And it's definitely no good for standing on the stage, because I perspire and it just goes flat and doesn't look at all glamorous. It won't hold a style, it doesn't hold a curl, it's just soft and feathery. It's nice to run your fingers through though ...

20

SEX, DRUGS AND ROCK-'N'-ROLL

❀

The success of 'I Will Survive', and the money and high-rolling lifestyle that came with it, brought me to a crossroads in my life. I could either go down the road of making out that life was a nonstop party, with champagne and cocaine flowing out of the taps – or I could start to do something about this aching void that had been growing inside me ever since I could remember, but particularly since my mother's death. As my popularity increased, I was working less and enjoying it more. But at home, just like when I was a little girl, I was being split in two.

❀

Between 1978 and 1982 I could feel myself sinking into the depth of degradation. We had so much money. As well as 'I Will Survive' being such a big hit, Linwood had had songs published by other artists in his publishing company. They never became really big hits, but you don't really need to have very big hits to make lots of money as a publisher. So he was making a lot of money, and I was making a lot of money.

We were hiring limousines and driving around with champagne in the back of the car, and you know, just having great fun. Linwood loved the fast cars, he loved the crazy, night and day parties that sometimes went on for weeks, and he loved all the attention he was getting from all sorts of women. And I was allowing things to happen that should never have happened, and that's all we'll say about that. People were getting far too deeply involved in our life, and I began to feel like just another one of the girls instead of his wife, and so the marriage wasn't doing well, and I didn't feel good about it at all.

We got in with the 'in crowd' and we met people who were bigger stars than we were. We were invited to wild parties, and we gave wild parties, and we got into marihuana – well, we'd been into marihuana for a long time – but we got a little more free with it. And then we got into cocaine.

I hated cocaine. But the terrible thing about cocaine is that cocaine doesn't care if you hate it. You must have more. Because it takes you up. Cocaine made me feel like someone was pushing me faster than I wanted to go. Some people like that. They like 'the rush'. But I'm really quite laid back, so it's a very irritating feeling for me. But to come down from it is even worse. You want to have more so you can stay up, until you've had so much that you've been 'up' so long, you must get some rest. That for me was usually after two or three days. I'd be up all night and all day for two or three days, and then I'd sleep all night and all day, and then I'd get up and start all over again, because everyone was doing it.

I did try. I kept trying to get off the merry-go-round and go to church. I'd stop, I'd say: 'This is it, I'm going to get back to being serious about God, like I was when I first came out of the hospital.'

I was trying to do all this in my own strength, because I didn't know anything about getting strength from God. I thought you were supposed to give God something, because God was giving you material things. I thought that God was hearing my list of wants and needs and desires every night, and the needs and desires of my friends every night, and for that he deserved me to do something for him. So I decided to be encouraging to other people, and a nice person. And I was going to pray – which for me then was like giving him my grocery list every night.

Don't get me wrong – I was enjoying the success I was having with my career. I was thankful for the success of my surgery, and wanted to share my gifts with people in a way that would have a lasting, positive effect, to become an encouraging role-model for them. In the years following 'I Will Survive' I released the albums *I Have a Right* and *Stories* – both with Freddy Perren – and *I Kind of Like Me*, which all included songs intended to help give people a good sense of self-worth and self-respect. I wrote some of the songs myself. Looking back, every song I ever wrote at that time was really a kind of love song to Linwood:

> *Don't read me wrong*
> *You have to know what I do, what I say*
> *I mean I'm sorry, Oh my love*
> *Some things I won't say*
> *Words get in the way*
> *Where love is the matter*
> *Don't read me wrong, I beg you*
> *Don't read me wrong, I tell you*
> *I'll make mistakes –*
> *For goodness sakes that's just exactly*
> *What they are.*
> *Don't read me wrong – forgive me*
> *Don't read me wrong – believe me*
> *Hurt's not the plan*
> *You'll understand if you will judge me with your heart.*

In 1981, on the album *I Kind of Like Me* I had the title song – 'I Kind of Like Me', and a rather racy song called 'Fingers in the Fire' – just to let you know I hadn't gone all the way religious!

> *Dimming lights*
> *Setting up a love scene just for me*
> *Ooh, Baby!*
> *I can plainly see*
> *You have done this act before.*
> *Yeah!*
> *The music's low*
> *What a great producer you could be*
> *Ooh, Baby!*
> *You think you're a lover*
> *I'll make you retire.*
> *Now don't put your fingers in the fire!*
> *Stop before you get 'em burned!*

Oh boy! The cover picture is pretty, but there's a pole coming out of my head. I also wrote: 'I Can Take the Pain' and 'I Love You 'cos'.

> *I love you 'cos*
> *You have so many sweet ways*
> *To bring me joy every day.*
> *I love you 'cos*
> *You ignore the faults in me*
> *And how you hurt*
> *Just when I hurt*
> *Although the doctor says there ain't no reason.*
> *I love you 'cos*
> *It's not just what you stand for*
> *Or what I think you are.*
> *I love you 'cos*
> *With you my love*
> *I feel the moon is near me*
> *And I could touch the stars.*

(and the last line I love best goes)

> *I love you 'cos*
> *When I am weak*
> *You're always strong*
> *But when you're down*
> *You're man enough to lean on your woman.*

I have such good albums. I mean, there are some songs that I thought were great then, when I was in the studio, and I'll hear them years later and think, 'That really was a nothing song'. But a lot of these songs I still look at and think, 'Whatever happened with these songs?' People can't buy what they don't hear.

❖

I would start going to church for a few months, but then I just couldn't stand being left out of all the good times Linwood and our friends were having, and also being an outsider at church, because I didn't know any other Christians. So I was always on my own. I couldn't stand that, so I'd be back smoking and drinking and going to the parties again, and getting upset with myself and feeling guilty. Then I would start going to church again. Every time my husband and friends would say, 'Oh, there she goes again. Oh well . . .' and my husband would say, 'That's nice, honey! You need that. That's good for you.'

Drugs and champagne. Looking back, it was like the Devil said: 'God, huh? I'll show you how godly you are, and who your God really is!'

I was loving it in a way, being so celebrated by everybody. But there was always that tug of the way my mother raised me, and my own growing need of God. But Linwood is a very hyper, up person. He had the same problem of not being able to rest, of not liking the 'down', but it wasn't so bad for him, because he liked the way it felt. It felt OK for him. He enjoyed being the life and soul of the party. I'm a wallflower, but he's the life of any party. He loved the attention. It was all great fun for him.

It got so bad that I wouldn't, or couldn't, pray at night, as I was always coming home very, very late. I didn't get to sleep until nearly morning or daybreak, and I was ashamed to pray. Especially since I knew that only hours later I'd probably be doing the same things again, the same things that I'd been doing the night before.

In 1982 I recorded the album *Gloria Gaynor*. It was on the Atlantic label, and was my tenth album. Linwood had written three songs for it. One was called 'Mackside' – it's a colloquial expression – 'on the mackside' means in the world of the mack, and a mack is a womanizer. It's all about the life of luxury of the mack, with Cadillacs and caviar and first-class airline tickets.

The god-fearing side of me slowly began to get the upper hand, and I was staying more and more in my room and ignoring the parties we would have. I thought that if I just went off and shut myself up in my room, they'd feel bad about it and go somewhere else and do it. But they didn't, not at first, because they always thought I was going to come back out.

When I realized that they weren't going to stop, I said, 'Look, I've had enough. I'm not having people partying half the night while

I'm trying to sleep.' I tried so hard to get Linwood to stop; I thought that because I was his wife, we were doing these things together, and when one of us said 'Enough' then both of us should stop.

He didn't agree with that. He began to go out and party, which meant him staying away a lot. But at least he knew now that I was getting serious.

They all began to shy away from me, and Linwood began to find it really hard to be with me. At one time he said he felt it was so bad, that he thought I was into the Devil. I guess all he felt coming from me was condemnation. And he thought 'God's not like that. God is a good God, and God doesn't condemn people and make them feel bad.' Anyway, he condemned me for condemning him, although I never intended to.

I can't honestly say that I wasn't a bit too zealous. I had had no 'discipling', I was alone with my faith, and the Holy Spirit. There was no coaching on how to witness to anybody else, I only knew that I was experiencing a wonderful life-changing God, and I wanted to share him with, most of all, my husband – who didn't want to know! They were not rejecting the message perhaps, but the messenger and the method.

21

SAVED!

In 1982 I got saved.

I went to a little Baptist church with my godmother one day. At the end of the service, they asked if anyone wanted to join the church and accept Christ as their Saviour. I felt I ought to join the church but I wasn't interested in accepting Christ as my Saviour, because I didn't even know what that meant. But I was thinking that God had been really good to me, and I'd been making a lot of money and so I should give God some commitment. As the people went forward to be accepted as members of the church, they were asked to say that they believed that Christ had lived and died for their sins, and risen again, and was forever interceding at the right hand of the Father. I was thinking: 'What on earth are they talking about? I don't know about any of that stuff. I mean, what is all that?'

I just left and went home, and it bothered me. So I dusted down a Bible that a girl had given me a few years before. She and I had somehow got onto the subject of religion, and I had not wanted her to think that I really didn't know anything about religion. In those days I always wanted people to think I knew about every-thing. Anyway, she must have realized that I didn't know much about it, because she had given me this study Bible. I'd felt as though she was trying to put me down in front of Linwood when she gave it to me, because she was another one who liked Linwood, although he will deny it. So I never read it. Once in a while I'd read a couple of psalms here and there. When I felt really down, I found a psalm that really bolstered you, like the 23rd Psalm. Psalms were really the only thing that I understood. Of course I'd read Genesis chapter 1 – fifteen times. I never got further than that, because I didn't understand what I was reading.

I opened up this Bible. I just let it fall open in the middle, and I said: 'God, I want to understand about this Jesus. I've been praying to you all my life. And I believe my prayers have been answered, and I never needed any Jesus to get my prayers answered . . .' (Looking back on that now, it sounds so selfish! But that's what I thought at that time.) 'So I want to know, who is this Jesus person really, and how come I've got to "know him" before I can join the church, and do I really need to know him before I can get in good with you? Because if you can talk to a preacher, and you can talk to a minister, then you can talk to me. I'm here. I'm listening. I want to know. I want to hear from *you*, because people make mistakes, people lie, people get confused, and I don't want to hear from the lady upstairs or the man down the hall. I want to hear it from you.'

So the Lord began to show me . . . I looked down at the Bible and it had opened at a section headed 'Harmonies of the Gospels and Prophecies Fulfilled' – which correlated the prophecies of the coming of the Messiah with the fulfilment in Christ.

I've learned that God deals with individuals one to one, and so since I am an analytical person, what he showed me first was an analysis of the times of the prophecies, and the time of the fulfilment. Because if somebody, ten years or less before Jesus was born, had said: 'The Messiah is coming and he's going to be born in such and such a place, and do such and such . . .' then I'd say, 'Well, Mary probably did that on purpose – tried to pretend that her son was the Messiah.' But when I saw that it had been prophesied seven *hundred* years before, and that many other prophecies had been made, anything up to a thousand years before, and how things that Mary could not have made happen had come true, and been fulfilled in Jesus, then I became convinced that Jesus was the Messiah, the Christ.

The Scripture that really 'saved' me was the one that says: 'For behold a virgin shall conceive and bear a Son, and shall call his name Emmanuel' (Isaiah 7:14). And it's repeated in Matthew, where it's explained that Emmanuel means God with Us. And I thought: 'Ooh! God with us! If Jesus is *God with us*, then – phew! that's heavy. That's really heavy. I guess he is important – I mean he's *God*.'

When I sat down at my dining room table and the Lord used that Scripture to draw me to salvation, I didn't immediately make the connection – that when I was a little girl, these were the first words I'd ever sung on the stage, performing the *Messiah* with the High School Glee Club. In fact it wasn't until nearly four years later, when I had some friends from the church over for Christmas, and we were getting ready to eat, and one of the girls wanted to read from the Bible. She read the Christmas story, and when she got to that part, I suddenly said: 'Can I sing that?' – that's when I first remembered the connection. It really makes it clear to me what the Bible means when it says: 'He who has ears to hear, let him hear.' I'd been singing those words for years, and yet I'd never heard them. I'd never really heard them.

❀

Somehow, I always believed that every word of the Bible was true. I never had any doubt about the Bible being true. Now I started to really go into it. I bought books on the Bible, books analysing the Bible prophecies, and books comparing the Bible prophecies with history, and I found that all of this is true.

This particular Scholar's Bible also had a section, Foundations in the Faith, teaching you that indeed Christ is God with us, that he did die for our sins, to reconcile us with God, and make us worthy of having a relationship with God.

So then I began to sit down at my dining room table every time I had the chance. Every evening I would spend an hour or two studying the Bible, and I began to buy other Bibles, and the Bible on tape.

The Holy Spirit led me through the Bible, and I got saved sitting at my own dining room table, just me and the Holy Spirit. For two years the Holy Spirit led me through the foundations of the faith. After a person accepts Christ as their Lord and Saviour and believes in their heart that God has raised Christ from the dead, they are saved, according to St Paul's letter to the Romans, chapter 10, verse 9. At that moment the Holy Spirit comes to live with and take care of that individual, to comfort, guide, empower and teach that person to be all that God has made him or her to be. So I feel very blessed, and unshakeable in my faith. I didn't get it from my aunt, my mother, my grandmother, the lady upstairs ... The Lord just began to talk to me. I really believe that.

I've heard people say, 'I talk to God. But I don't hear him say anything to me!' Well I think there are two things that are necessary to be saved. One is that you have got to be ready to hear and accept God's truth, and submit to it whatever it means: whatever it means that you have to give up, whatever it means that you have to change, you have to be willing – not necessarily able – but you have to be *willing* to do whatever God says you need to do. And that's where I was at that point.

I was tired of my life. I had everything that I could possibly want. I had money, I had cars, I had the love of my husband, I had so-called friends, but there was a void, a God-shaped void, that only God was going to be able to fill. And I was ready for it to be filled. That's why I was saved and other people, who say they talk to God and he doesn't answer them, are not. You've got to be willing to hear and receive the truth. Christ said: 'I am the Truth' so if you receive Christ, you must receive the truth. And speaking from experience – that can be painful as well as joyful.

The second thing is, being saved means being born again. In order to be born again, you first have to die. Your old self has to die, and you have to let it die. Most of us want to hang on to our faults and weaknesses, because we think they make us what we are. Without them, we think, we'd be nothing. But behind all your faults and weaknesses are great gifts and strengths that you only discover as you let your faults and weaknesses go.

I believe I was born again that first day that I sat down with the Bible. But I don't know what day it was because, although I knew that what I was doing was significant, it never crossed my mind that it mattered what time or day or year it was or anything. Sometimes now I wish I knew, because it's nice to have another birthday! I do know it was 1982.

❀

After I had been studying the Bible on my own, for two years, I began to want to go to church again. This time I wanted to find a church that was closer to home, one where I believed that I could learn and grow and really belong.

I thought maybe I should go back to my grandmother's church, that I'd gone to as a child. I remember walking up to it feeling 'This is home' and I walked in and thought: 'Oh Glory! this is wonderful! This is it!'

Nobody spoke to me – before or after the service. And the next Sunday the same thing. So I thought, maybe I ought to say something to them. And I stood up and I told them that I had come, and I wanted to join the church, and they said: 'Oh, that's wonderful! Praise the Lord, Sister!' And they gave me an application form where I could sign my name and address. And I told them that I was a Christian, but I didn't have a church.

The next thing I got from them in the mail was a big pile of offering envelopes. And that was all I ever heard from them. I went two more Sundays but still nobody said anything to me, nobody greeted me, people never sat near me, or if they did, they didn't say anything. The preacher would say a Scripture, and then he'd go on ahooping and ahollering, and I never knew what he was saying or how it related to the Scripture he'd read and least of all to me. This was not the answer. I started looking for another church.

❧

In 1984 I went to a Christian Convention at the Nassau Coliseum, in New York, given by a pastor, a television evangelist named Fred Price, where I got baptized in the Holy Spirit. As I've said, I was born again sitting at my dining room table at home. But now I was *publicly* baptized in the Holy Spirit, and made a public declaration that I believed in Christ and accepted him as my Lord and Saviour. The Holy Spirit comes upon you – we say 'comes upon' but what he does is endue you with power to do what he wants you to do, as well as to be what he wants you to be.

I had gone to the Convention hoping to get Linwood saved, but instead I got baptized in the Holy Spirit myself! Linwood was very pleased for me. He said he could see I was really enjoying whatever it was.

A few nights later, I was praying about what to do about Linwood and everything, and I suddenly thought I should anoint his side of the bed. Linwood had been away for a couple of nights. I got up and I got some oil that I had blessed, and I anointed his side of the bed. I also went into his closet and I anointed his shoes and his hat and his clothes, and I prayed over them, and I claimed the spirit of the one that wore those clothes, and the one that lay on that side of the bed, for Jesus, and I just prayed for his salvation.

He came home later that night, but he didn't get into the bed. He slept on the couch. He wouldn't use anything from that closet for days. He slept on the carpet, he slept on the chaise longue and the couch. He couldn't or wouldn't go out, I guess because he couldn't go into that closet where his favourite clothes were. So he never got anointed!

I thought it would have worked if he had only changed his clothes or lain down on the bed, but I have since learned that although prayer and anointing can create a thirst, they can't force anyone to drink who doesn't want to. God never violates the gift he gave us of free will.

What I did – or tried to do – for Linwood was spiritual. So I can fully believe that the spiritual beings we call demons kept him from getting into the bed. They instilled a fear in him about getting into the bed. He probably didn't himself know why he didn't want to get into bed. He probably just thought he didn't want to be near me. When evil spirits speak to you and make suggestions to you, unless you are a spiritual person, you don't want to admit that these things exist. So you accept these thoughts as your own, and you follow through on them. Unless you read the Bible, you don't know how to deal with them. You have no defence and you'd rather think that an enemy does not exist if you have no defence against them.

I still hadn't found a church to belong to. One day a friend called whom I hadn't seen for nearly ten years – my childhood friend, Grear. Some years earlier I had run into her and she had told me she was 'saved' but at that time I had had no idea what she meant by it. This time when she called me, I told her that I had become a Christian, and that I was 'saved' and had been baptized in the Holy Spirit and was looking for a church to belong to. She said: 'Thank God!' She had been praying for me for seven years! She told me that she belonged to the Assemblies of God, a Pentecostal church, who believed that the Bible was the inspired Word of God, from Genesis to Revelation. That was good enough for me. She gave me the names of four churches in the neighbourhood.

I went through the list, and I prayed over the list: 'Oh God, help me to go to the one that's good. I've had enough of running in and out of different churches. Now, God, which one do you want me to go to? I'm going to pick one and I just pray that that will be the one that you want me to go to.'

I started to choose one because it was closest, but then I thought 'Na.' Then I chose one that was close to my sister, but then I thought 'Na!' Then I chose another one for no particular reason, or so I thought.

On the next Sunday, I drove off to find it. It was on a street called Kennedy Boulevard, in North Bergen. And when I got there – it was an empty lot. Then I found out that Kennedy Boulevard goes through three different small cities. I searched up and down this street that ran through three cities, the number starting anew in each city. But none had a church at the address that was on this piece of paper. There was an empty lot, or a narrow space between two buildings, or a derelict building, but there was never a church.

Driving along, on the way back, I said: 'Lord, did I hear you wrong, or what? I mean, I know you have a sense of humour but, with all due respect, I'm truly not amused at nine o'clock in the morning, riding up and down the street in the rain, trying to find this building. So tell me something.'

Then I noticed that she had given me a telephone number for the church, so I stopped and called the number. I didn't get any answer, so I went on back home.

When I got home, I tried calling again. This time I got the pastor's wife, who told me that I had gone to the right place but that they were in the process of rebuilding the church. In the meantime they were carrying on their meetings at a Senior Citizens' building nearby.

So the following Sunday I went, and I asked God to give me a sign if this was the church that he really wanted me to be in. I got there, and nothing happened. I mean, I enjoyed the service, but I didn't get any particular sign. But when the service was over a bunch of people came to me and said: 'We see that you're new. We hope you enjoyed it! Did you enjoy it?' And they were so happy and cheerful and welcoming, and they laughed and talked with me and offered me refreshments and all this sort of thing. So I talked with them. I had come by taxi, and eventually I asked them where was the telephone so I could call a taxi to go home.

'Oh no! You don't need a taxi. Don't worry about it. Somebody will take you home.' Two girls drove me and they asked me if I wanted to come back that evening. I thought, 'Going to church twice in one day is really fanatical', so I wasn't interested in going back. But they insisted that I would love it if I came back. So I said, 'OK.'

During the evening service they had testimonies – people stood up and talked about their faith. I had never done that before, but I felt I should do this.

I stood up, and I said, 'Um. Well. I got mugged coming into church today.'

They said, 'What!?'

'Yeah! I got mugged by the Holy Spirit!'

I explained to them that I had asked the Lord for a sign that evening. In the morning I'd asked for a sign, and I had thought it was a sign that they had all been so nice and friendly and offered to take me home, and all of that, but I had really wanted an undeniable sign. I had been saying that to the Lord when I came in that evening and, as I was saying it, I was sitting down putting my handbag down on the floor. I got to my feet with the spirit of laughter just bubbling over. And nobody paid any attention! So I had thought, 'Yeah. This is the place.'

They all laughed. They thought that was ever so funny. So I knew that that was the right church for me to be in. I became a member and stayed in that church for five years. I learned a lot, and grew in the faith in leaps and bounds.

Now I was grounded in my faith, and nobody could shake me, and my friends were beginning to realize that this was not just another episode of Gloria going off to get a dose of God, and calm her conscience long enough to come back and get into garbage again. By this time, everybody knew that I was seriously committed to the Lord.

I had met the Lord, and I was getting strength from the Lord, and there was no way I was going to turn back just to be friends with them. Every now and then I'd go and be with the group but I was with them, not of them any more. And they felt the difference. I knew that it was not enough of a difference, but they did feel the difference.

I was still drinking a little wine, still smoking marihuana. I was telling myself that when I drank and when I smoked (especially when I smoked) I could get on a higher plane, and be closer to God. How you can lie to yourself!

Later on in 1984 I went to Europe, to England. I went out to a big dinner with Malcolm Feld, whose agency always booked me in England, and Gina Maher, the actress, who was his fiançée then and is today his wife and mother of his two dear little daughters. They have both become very dear friends. Gina is a Catholic, and Malcolm is Jewish. I met them in their home first, and I was telling her how she ought to pray for him, but she wasn't into it. But I really wanted to minister Christ to them, to him especially, so they could get together on this thing and I could get them both saved.

On our way out to the hotel where the dinner was being held, I thought to myself, 'When we get to where we're going, I'm not going to drink, because most people think that real Christians shouldn't drink.' But when we got to the door of this place, they were standing at the door with glasses of champagne. And of course, that was my drink. I loved champagne. I even had it in my contract rider, that I must have champagne in the dressing room. I would drink it after the show. I thought I was really good, because I never drank it before my show. I drank after my show.

So when they offered me champagne at the door, I just took it, out of habit. They didn't let your glass get empty. We were milling round talking while they got the tables set, and my glass was never empty. By the time I sat down I was already a little bit tipsy. They had wine on the tables. So I called a waiter over, and said, 'Excuse me, but this is wine, and I've been drinking champagne. Do you think you could get me a glass of champagne?'

And he said, 'Oh, of course, Madam, no problem'.

So he came back, gave me the glass, and I sipped it and said, 'This isn't champagne, it's wine.'

So that was chance number one to quit, but I didn't. I called him back. In fact, in the end, I called him back three times, and finally he came over with the bottle of champagne and said, 'Is this what you were drinking?'

And I said, 'Yes, it is.'

And so he poured me a drink and said, 'Do you want me to keep filling the glass or do you want me to leave the bottle?'

I said, 'Leave the bottle.' I didn't want him to lose it somewhere!

Meanwhile, I was speaking about Christ to a girl who was sitting beside me. And I was talking like this: 'Jeeshush ish really the one. You know whad I'm shaying? He'sh *really* God!'

The next morning, when I woke up, I thought, 'There you sat, speaking about the Lord with such fervour and conviction, the only girl – the only person – sitting at the table with a whole bottle of liquor in front of you – what a representation of Christ that must have been to that woman!'

I fell on my knees and said, 'Lord, forgive me. I am so sorry. And if you would take away from me the taste for alcohol, for champagne, I will never have another drink as long as I live.'

And that was the last time I took a drink. The Lord miraculously took away from me the taste for any kind of alcohol, cigarettes and marihuana. The very next night I had no desire for any of those things. None whatever. When I left the dressing room after the show that night, those two full bottles of champagne were still sitting unopened on the table.

22

A NEW SONG

It was 1984. I was in church one day (we were still in the Senior Citizens' building) and a woman stood up and started speaking in tongues.

Now earlier that year, at the Christian Convention at the Nassau Coliseum given by Fred Price, I had been baptized in the Holy Spirit, and had begun speaking in tongues, so I was very familiar with it. I had even read and studied in the Scholar's Bible about the interpretation of tongues, but I didn't myself have that gift. I'd heard people interpret what other people speaking in tongues were saying, but I'd just stood there and listened.

This time I felt involved, but irritated, because I could not understand what she was saying. Then I felt two hands on my shoulders pressing me firmly down to the floor.

I remembered going to church with my grandmother, when old ladies – they were probably about forty years old, but they were old to me! – would get 'happy' and start shouting and hallelujahing and fall down; but it seemed to me as a child that they would never fall until a handsome man came round, and then they would fall into his arms! I thought it was so ridiculous.

Now here I was falling down on the floor. There was no handsome man, and I wasn't shouting 'Hallelujah' or anything but there I was, on the floor. Nobody took the least bit of notice. They must have seen it before, and knew what was happening.

Just before I had been protesting in my spirit about the speaking in tongues. I was saying, 'I do not know what this person is talking about. I don't have any interpretation of tongues. I just don't understand.' So when I fell down on the floor I thought, 'This means "shut up and listen." ' So I stayed there. I couldn't get up. I didn't even want to get up.

Then somebody started speaking in English, and I'll never, ever forget the words:

'You have been seeking guidance. If you will just choose to follow me, I will take you to greater heights than you have ever thought possible. I will put a new song in your heart.'

When that was finished I felt released, so I got up and was dusting myself off. I said to my girlfriend who was standing next to me, 'Well, I wonder who that was for.' And she just looked at me and laughed, and I laughed, and we just went on with the service. But I treasured the words in my heart.

A year later, the church had moved into the new building. The same woman stood up and started speaking in tongues again.

Again I thought, 'What are you saying, Lord?' but this time I was smiling, I felt so blessed, but I was saying, 'I don't know what you are saying! I don't have interpretation of tongues! What are you saying?' Then a voice said:

'You have been seeking guidance. If you will just choose to follow me, I will take you to greater heights than you have ever thought possible. I will put a new song in your heart.'

The same words. The exact same words. And I thought, 'My Lord! What is happening? Why am I hearing this again?'

The next day, Monday, I went into New York for something, I can't remember what, and on my way back I was passing by a Christian Bookstore. I thought about a book that I wanted to buy. I double-parked my car. You do not double-park your car in New York, because it'll get towed. But I thought I'd be very, very quick. I ran into the store thinking, 'I'll quickly get this book, pay for it, and be out in no time before the police can come along.' I'm standing in line, and I hear the Lord say to me, 'Go over to the music section'. I think, 'I don't have time' and he says, 'Go over to the music section'

and I say, 'I can't do that. They're going to tow my car away.' 'Go to the music section!'

So I went over to the music section. And I'm standing there in front of the tapes with my hands on my hips, and I realize later that I was 'sassing' the Lord, as we say in America. 'OK, now what? I'm here. So what? What? What? Just what?' And suddenly I see, in the gospel section, a tape titled *I Will Survive*.

And I thought, 'Oh God! Somebody's written a gospel song called 'I Will Survive' and I'm going to hate it. God wants me to sing it, but I know I'm going to hate it.'

You know how you feel, when you first become a Christian, that God's going to send you off to minister in the jungle or something? And you're going to hate it? I thought exactly that. I thought, 'God's given me this song – and I'm going to *hate* it!'

They had tape recorders there, so I listened to the song and it was the story of my life. I bought my book, bought the tape, got back outside, and thanked the Lord for letting his angels stand by my car, which was still there.

I took the song home and I learned it. I played it for Linwood, and he thought it was absolutely beautiful. The artist was Cynthia Clawson. I think the writer's name is Galliardi.

Although I found the song in 1985, it was not until 1990 that I finally got an opportunity to record it and include it on an album. The album went gold in Italy, but it hasn't been released anywhere else yet. But I sang it everywhere. I sang it in my church, and I sang it in Britain at Kensington Temple and at South Lee, my friend Bebe's church. I will definitely record it again as soon as I do the new gospel album that I'm planning to do very soon now.

A year later I was in bed one night, and I thought that someone woke me. At first I said, 'What? What is it?' because I thought it was Linwood. Someone said, 'You have to write a song.' I opened one eye and looked at the clock and said, 'It's four-thirty in the morning! Are you crazy?' And then I turned over to see if he was dreaming or something, and realized that he wasn't there. He was away for the weekend. But I still felt this compulsion to get up and write a song.

So I got up and I thought, 'Now, if I write this song down, I'm not going to remember the melody in the morning.' I don't even know why I thought that, because I'd never written songs with melodies before. I only ever wrote lyrics.

But this time I thought, 'I won't remember the melody, so I'd better get a tape recorder. It'll be quicker.'

I still didn't know what I was going to sing. I sat down at the dining room table with the tape recorder, and the first words that came out of my mouth were '*You're not alone. Jesus is with you.*'

I completed the song, and went back to bed, and tried to get back to sleep, but I felt I had to get up again. So I got up again an l went back to the tape recorder and sang into it two more songs. One was called 'Don't You Wonder?' which asks the question 'Don't you wonder why Christians are so happy?' and the other song is called 'Live for Jesus'. I went back to bed.

When I woke up the next morning I went to the tape recorder and played back the songs. I liked all the lyrics very much, but I didn't have much confidence in the melodies. So I wrote the lyrics down, put the tape away and didn't think any more about it.

❀

About a year later, when I was in England in 1988, I met a young man, Frank Collins, who was doing some backing for me, and who had some songs that he wanted me to listen to. So he came by my hotel the next day and played them for me. They were all love songs, and one was called 'The Answer'. The melody and the arrangement had an American style gospel sound, and I thought the title was great. I said, 'That sounds like a gospel song!' He said that people often said that about his music.

I said, 'Well, if that's the case, I have a couple of songs that I'd like you to put a melody to and arrange for me.' I gave him just the lyrics of the songs I'd written that night at four in the morning. I told him that if and when I did my gospel album, I'd probably like to include his song, 'The Answer', with the lyrics changed to make it into a Christian song. He was really happy about that.

A few months later Frank sent me the tape of his arrangements. I listened to them and, lo and behold, they were the same melodies!

The Lord had given him the same melodies as he had given me. I couldn't believe it. I got the original tape and played it, and they really were virtually the same melodies. There were a couple of notes that were different, because I had sung the harmony to what he had written. But they were the same melodies! It was really extraordinary.

I have no doubt that the Lord has given me these songs, and one day I shall record them.

In 1988 Ears and Eyes, an English record company, put together a show, and we invited 150 members of the press. The aim was to launch me out of secular music and into gospel music. I did the first half of the show singing my secular hits, and the second part singing gospel songs. That is where I first sang the two 'I Will Survive's together. I said to the audience: 'I've been telling you 'I will survive', but I've done you an injustice: I've never told you *how* I've managed to survive, how I will survive, and how you also can survive.' Then I sang the gospel 'I Will Survive'. That was the last song – I went off singing 'I will survive, I will survive, I will survive . . .'

Looking ahead is just a little bit easier
When you look at where you've been.
I can believe that we can move mountains
'Cos he's carried me through
Every valley I knew.
If it wasn't for Christ
I don't know where I'd be.
I just know that for me
I can rest in the promise of his love.

I will survive
He gave me life
I stand beside the Crucified One
I can go on
I will be strong
For my strength to live is not my own
I will survive.

Sometimes it seems the pain of life
Will take over me,
That fear I'll lose again –
Then I realize to fight to the finish
I'll just lean on the Son
'Cos he's second to none
And the battle is already won.

I will survive
He gave me life
I stand beside the Crucified One
I can go on
I will be strong
For my strength to live is not my own
I will survive.

And with his love to guide me I know
That the past is far behind me
And his Spirit now reminds me
That through the changes in my life
I will survive.

Just like the lily in the winter snow
Waiting for Spring
I face the darkness
But I'm not alone
I have the light
And I will grow
And I will sing
And I must sing

I will survive
He gave me life
I stand beside the Crucified One
I can go on
I will be strong

For my strength to live is not my own
I will survive
I will survive
I will survive
I can go on
I will be strong
For my strength to live is not my own
I will survive
I will survive
I will survive.

23

GLASGOW

Around 1987 I went to Glasgow to do a couple of nights performances in a hotel. I was going to be there for about four or five days, to do some interviews and that kind of thing, as well as to perform. I was alone. Linwood was busy back in New Jersey. I had been in England with Malcolm Feld, my agent there. Linwood was always all right about letting me go there, because he knew Malcolm and Gina would take care of me. I'd often stayed in their home.

In Glasgow I'd checked into the hotel, had a little dinner and gone to bed. I woke up the next morning feeling absolutely miserable. I was very weak. I didn't have sniffles or a runny nose or anything like that, but I had a headache and my body ached from head to toe.

I managed to get to the telephone to call downstairs and ask them to send me a doctor. I said, 'Lord, you've shown me so many of the wonders of the world and you've guided me through so much – am I going to die here, all alone in this Holiday Inn hotel room in Glasgow? Is this the end you've had planned for me?'

The doctor came a couple of hours later. He said, 'Oh dear. You're not well at all. It's a virus. It'll last four to seven days and you'll just have to let it work through. There's absolutely nothing to be done about it.

I had a show that night. I wondered how on earth I could get through it. I began to pray for the Lord to heal me. I prayed and kind of hummed praises to the Lord. I tried to get through my vocalization (because I always vocalize before I go on stage) but I didn't have the strength to do any of it. I read the Bible and prayed and proclaimed all the promises of God in the Bible.

I decided to wear an outfit that didn't take any preparation. It was all sequins so it wasn't going to get wrinkled or anything. Then I began to prepare the list of songs I was going to do for the show. One was called 'I Give You Jesus'. A line in the song is 'If your body is in pain, and your health you can't regain, you need someone . . . I give you Jesus.' And while I was thinking about that song, the Enemy said to me, "Are you going to sing that song? You're going to sing to the people: 'If your body is in pain, and your health you can't regain . . ." while you're feeling like you're feeling?'

And I said, 'Yes I am. First of all, I'm not going to be feeling like I'm feeling by the time I get down there. The Lord's going to heal me. I'm going to be fine. And even if I do feel like this, I'm still going to sing it.'

I always believe that if you pray for healing, and you believe it (like the Bible says, 'pray in faith, believing') God is going to do whatever it is you ask him to do. And I believe that if you don't get whatever it is you've asked for, it's for some reason that you don't understand. I believe it's always on you, because God is faithful to all of his promises, and wants us all to walk in divine health. He's always ready, willing and able, to answer your prayers. I don't believe God ever wants you to be sick.

By the time I had to get ready to do the show I was feeling really, really miserable I managed to shower and change, and just about crawl downstairs. I was so weak I couldn't hold the microphone in my hand. I never usually work with a microphone on the stand, but I had to this time, and I just stood there with my arms by my side. It took all the strength I could muster to get my voice out.

I didn't talk much in between. I was always taught it's unprofessional to tell people that you're sick, so I didn't make any excuses to the audience. I did the show and then went off the stage.

Back in my room I fell down on the bed and began to cry and ask God why he had not healed me. I have to admit I felt a little let down. I wasn't angry or anything like that, but I just didn't understand.

Then the Lord said, 'I wanted the *Enemy* to see that you would praise me even in adversity. And I wanted *you* to know that, when you sing a song about me, and people are blessed, it's not because you sing beautifully, it's not because you sing with fervour and conviction and you mean the words to the song, because I don't need you to do any of that. I don't need you to make grand testimonies, I don't need you to sing well. I don't even need you to *be* well. I just need you to be willing to be used.'

I was satisfied with that answer, and I got up and crawled into the shower and went to bed. I woke up the next morning as fresh as a daisy, completely well, like I'd never been sick!

Pastor Bernard says that sometimes we say to the Lord, 'Why me, Lord? Why do I have to go through all these problems, why do I have to have all these trials and tribulations? Why me, Lord? Why do I have to suffer like this?' And God says, 'Well, because that's the way you are. It's not me! I don't want you to go through all of that, but you just don't seem to learn!'

The doctor did not say it was a twenty-four-hour virus. He said that it would last from four to seven days, according to my symptoms, and I expect he knew what he was talking about. I'm not asking you to make up your minds whether that was a healing miracle or not, although that's what I believe it was. The important point is that I got a lesson out of it: one that I never have and never shall forget. The Lord really put me in my place. We can tend to start thinking that it's what we've done, our talents and gifts, our goodness that is bringing people to the Lord. But it isn't. We are just his instruments, and we have to learn to be just that so the Lord of the universe can accomplish what he wants to accomplish through us.

A year after my Christmas concert in London, with Michael Wakelin of the BBC's Religious Programmes producing the broadcast for Radio 2, Michael flew over to New Jersey to talk to me about my presenting a weekly radio show on Radio 2 in the UK called 'The Gospel Train'. It's one of the things I'm most pleased about having done in my musical life. I presented the programme for four years, playing gospel records by traditional and contemporary gospel artists, and some of what I called 'vintage' gospel from artists as early as 1914.

It was my best yet opportunity to share the knowledge and love of Christ with my fans in Britain. I had already discovered that in the UK some Christians can be somewhat conservative. I think that at first, in their judgment, I was associated with disco and show business, and was not a fellow Christian and church member. I did six series of 'The Gospel Train' between 1989 and 1993, and two wonderful Christmas concerts at the London Hippodrome in 1991 and 1992, when I had the opportunity to work with some of the best musicians and singers in Britain.

I recorded my last two 'Gospel Train' series at the beginning of 1993. I'm sorry I'm not doing it any more, but they wanted someone who could spend several weeks in Britain travelling round the country with live shows, rather than recording links and playing records in a studio. I just didn't have enough time for that. I miss it though, working with Michael Wakelin and Tanya Astley and the whole BBC team, who were all wonderful Christians, and I would be very happy to do it again.

I wasn't always familiar with the music they wanted me to play. People in Britain don't sing exactly the same gospel music as we do in the States. Our nephew, George, Cynthia's son, who lives and works with Linwood and me now and is a great asset to the business, thinks gospel music on both sides of the Atlantic is almost always at least a year out of date. He says that if people sing a gospel rap number, for instance, it sounds like the last secular rap hit, but never like the next rap hit. I wonder if he's right? Come on, fellow gospel artists – we've got to change all of that!

24

A NEW CHURCH

By 1988 I'd been going to the Assemblies of God church for four years, and I had learned a lot, and grown a lot. But they didn't teach you in any really practical way how to minister to the unsaved. They talked about it, and encouraged you to do it, but they didn't let you know how to convince without condemning, or how to allow the Holy Spirit to win people over. One day they would say you should share the Lord with your family and friends, and the next day they would say you've got to let God save them. It didn't make any practical sense to me. I didn't know how to make that effective in my life. They didn't seem to know how to tell me.

I found out later that the minister there had been saved since he was five years old, and all his family were Christians. What could he know about dealing with the world where Linwood was coming from?

While I was in England in 1988 when I met Frank Collins, he told me he knew Candi Staton, the celebrated gospel singer, and her husband, because he used to work with her husband years ago. Candi's husband had called Frank on the telephone recently and told him that he was now saved. And he said, 'Well, did you know Gloria Gaynor is a born-again Christian? Maybe you guys should get together.'

While I was in England I went regularly to my best friend Bebe's church in Catford, at South Lee, and was received there with great warmth and love. I sang the new gospel 'I Will Survive' for them.

When I was about to leave they all prayed for me, and one gentleman said that he heard the Lord saying that I was going to meet a couple who would be instrumental in my ministry, and one of them would have red hair. But I wasn't to look for the red hair, I was to recognize them by their love for the Lord.

I came back home, and I called Candi Staton. We talked on the telephone, and I told her that I wanted to get into gospel music. She said that she would send me some backing tapes of gospel music, with the song on one side, and just the backing track on the other. I could learn the song, and then have the backing track to perform it with. She sent about ten of them, and also several of her own albums. And when I opened the package and looked at the cover – she had red hair. Of course she had always had red hair, but I'd forgotten.

I called her to thank her and told her what the man in the church in England had said. I said I had a growing feeling that I was no longer in the right church for me. She said she went to a church in Manhattan, that held its meetings in the Salvation Army theatre, and she'd be pleased if I came along and we could meet.

As soon as I walked into the church I felt 'This is home.' Everyone was singing praises, and it seemed that they were all happy and loved the Lord. The pastor came out and said, 'Good morning' and everyone said, 'Good morning!' back. He said, 'How in the world are you?' and they all called back 'Blest in Jesus' name!'

I found Candi, who introduced me to the pastor. They sat me down in the front. Candi introduced me to the church, and everybody was so pleased I had become a Christian – because many of them knew me – and was now going to sing for the Lord. I sang 'I Give You Jesus' for them. Afterwards we went to Candi's mother-in-law's house, and we spent quite a few hours together.

I went back to that church a couple of times after that, and then called Pastor Bernard, and told him I wanted to join. He said, 'Why?' I told him that the pastor was really nice in the church where I was, and I loved him and respected him, but I wasn't

learning any more, and I wasn't getting help in how to minister to
Linwood. I felt I could learn more in his church. I had already
learned so much in the two weeks I'd been there, and felt I could
continue to learn and grow.

He said, 'OK. Fine. I just wanted to find out if you were flaky.
Because we've got enough of our own flakes!' He asked me to
write a letter to my pastor, to tell him I was leaving and why, and to
give him his name. He said all the ministries, all the churches, every
minister that God has called was needed, and if a minister had got
a problem, that was causing his parishioners to leave, he needed
to know.

My pastor understood. So I joined the new church, and I've
been there ever since.

When you come to my church, the Christian Life Centre, you have
to sit in the ministry for at least a year before you are able to operate
any kind of ministry yourself. And you are required to take a
spiritual growth course to make sure that you understand what the
church believes and what the Bible teaches. Then you won't
disseminate anything that's contrary to the Bible.

After I had been going there for just over a year, we moved into
the new building and I was accepted to join the choir. When I first
started going there were approximately 540 members, and we were
holding our meetings at the Salvation Army Auditorium in
Manhattan, having moved from our old place in Brooklyn. They
had bought a supermarket in Brooklyn, and were in the process of
converting it into a church, so construction was going on. Pastor
Bernard believed the Lord had told him to stay in Brooklyn in a
very bad area which is of course where churches are needed.

In the five years that have passed since then, we have grown to
over 5,000 members. It was then, and still is, over fifty per cent male,
which is a great drawing power on the community because it shows
strength; there are a lot of teenagers, and people from say sixteen,
seventeen to thirty-five. So it's quite a young congregation although,
of course, we've also got a lot of old people and a lot of babies!

We now have to have three services, at eight o'clock, ten o'clock and twelve o'clock every Sunday. The choir is broken up into three parts, so nobody has to be in church for all three services and we rotate, so nobody has to get up at five in the morning every Sunday. But on the last Sunday of the month, the whole choir, is there for all three services, and the choir ministers to the congregation. The rest of the Sundays we really just lead the congregation in praise and worship. On choir Sunday we still have praise and worship with the congregation, but there are one or two songs that the choir really ministers.

On the second Sunday we have baby dedications, usually by Elder Pointer, a lovely annointed assistant pastor. We don't believe in baby baptism, because the Bible says that baptism is an outward expression of having accepted Christ as your Lord and Saviour. A baby can't do that, so Pastor Bernard says if you haven't voluntarily accepted Christ before Baptism, you don't get baptized, you just get wet. We have adult baptism and baby dedications in which we call the parents and godparents to take responsibility for the child's spiritual upbringing having dedicated the child to Christ for his protection. You don't want a child growing up thinking it's already been done. You've still got to make a decision on your own. The second Sunday is always very moving and lovely.

On the first Sunday we generally have Communion. Once in a while something will supersede the Communion, but it's always through the moving of the Holy Spirit. The Lord has told the pastor to do something else, and he's sensitive to the time and doesn't want the twelve o'clock service ending at three, so we don't have Communion. The Lord doesn't say 'Do it every first Sunday or every third Sunday.' He just says 'As often as you do it . . .'

The pastor calls all of the ministry people to the front, and he and his wife, Karen, minister Communion to them – including the choir. Generally he turns around to the choir, who sit very near the pulpit, which is actually a stage, because the Sanctuary doubles as a theatre. He'll serve the first row of the choir, and he and his wife minister to all of the ushers, and then they minister to the rest of the church. They all take trays, go to the end of each row and give them to the first person. Then that person takes the tray and gives it to the next person, and the second person serves them. Then the second person gives it to the third person, and they minister to them. It goes all the way down to the other end of the row. We serve each other.

Pastor Bernard says what it all means, and encourages us to repent and ask forgiveness for anything we haven't yet asked forgiveness for while we were being served. I always read Psalm 51 while it's happening.

We all love and are so proud of our pastor. He really talks to you. He'll be saying something like 'And so this is what's meant by that . . . and I've got to stop.' And you'll hear a groan – 'Aaah!' You always hear that, because we never want him to stop. No matter how long you've been there, you never want him to stop. Every service is like a sumptuous meal.

He must be about forty-two. He says, 'I'm definitely not a typical preacher. I'm not short . . .' (Well, he's not tall!) 'I'm not fat, I'm not bald, I don't have a paunch and I drive a Harley Davidson motorcycle.' (His wife gave him one for his birthday last year! He's terrifically nonconforming!)

We always bring notebooks. The church is the only institute of knowledge that people go to with no tools: no books, no pads, no pens, no paper. You always know the members of our church because they have a notepad, a pen, or even a computer. People take their laptops. You take notes, because you don't want to miss anything. Our pastor says, 'The Bible is not a religious book. The Bible is a book of patterns and principles upon which God has intended man to construct a proper social structure. But these patterns and principles, like soap, will not do you any good, unless you apply them.'

Each service holds 1,100 people, but it's always over-full. We have a tent where people wait for the next service. They start lining up for the eight o'clock service at six, six-thirty in the morning.

We have a church school. From the first to twelfth grade – twelve years of education can be had there. When we have built the new Sanctuary, the new church will be called the Christian Cultural Centre and will hold a 10,000 seat sanctuary; we've grown so much in five years, there's no sense in building a church for 5,000 people now. It will have a theatre playhouse, it will have a

hotel (because we get people from three States and they often need
to stay overnight). It will have a restaurant because, if people have
been there all day, they want to eat. It will have an office block, so
that we can get people from the secular business world, and disseminate Christian principles there. We will have underground parking
for 5000 cars. The site we are on now will be an expanded school –
we'll use the whole building for the school.

❧

Every Christmas we have a play, and for the last three years we've
done the same play written, produced and acted by the congregation, members of the choir and members of our Creative Arts
Department. The costume designers and seamstresses are all
members of the congregation, as are the set designers and set
builders.

The pastor said that the Lord had given him a vision for the
church, and it was a musical vision. In order to make sure that he
was getting it right, he gave us what he called 'a spiritual gifts assessment' and found that we already had in the church everything we
could possibly need to put together a professional production.

So we put on a play called *Christ Lives After All*. Pastor Bernard
believes in doing everything for the Lord with the spirit of excel-
lence: no second-hand scraps of old curtains or hand-me-down
costumes – everything was made new. He also believes that God's
will done God's way will never lack God's supply. So what God
calls you to do something, he's going to make sure you have everything you need to do it with.

The production, to all intents and purposes, is a Broadway play.
We have a playbill, in which all the local businesses and suchlike
advertise, just like on Broadway; we have tickets, just like on
Broadway; the seats are numbered and you get seated by ushers. We
have everything that they have on Broadway, plus the Holy Spirit
for all!

The play is about a family who are living in the millennium and
telling their grandchildren how it was before the Rapture, and after
the Rapture, during the Tribulation period. We believe in Before
Tribulation Rapture. In the first year I played the part of Martyred

Deedee, who had been left behind at the Rapture, and was martyred. The other two years I haven't been home to rehearse, so they haven't been able to depend on me, so my part was given to someone else.

In the play, someone tries to minister to Deedee. They give her tapes, but she just doesn't want to know. But when the Rapture came and she was left behind she started to listen to those tapes and accepted Christ. She refused the Mark of the Beast under torture, and was beheaded.

I couldn't believe it when I first saw my make-up in the mirror – my face looked swollen, my lips were hanging off, my head was bloody, my hair was wild as though I'd stuck my finger in an electric plug. The blood and the scars were amazing. When I came on I heard a child crying, 'Oh! Mom! What have they done to that lady?' I sang a song called 'Christ Lives After All', which is the name of the play.

I'd love to do it again. I'd like to have a bigger part. They gave me that part because they knew that I wouldn't be around very much, and there wasn't so much for me to learn. And the understudy, Marilyn Harewood, who's been doing the part ever since, is marvellous. In fact, I would say she does it better than me. She certainly sings the song better than I do, she really does.

❧

We have intercessory prayer, Bible study, spiritual growth classes, and then we have singles ministry. They go off on trips to the Poconos Mountains. We have couples ministries, and they also go off on trips together; the choir from time to time goes away, ministers to one another and has seminars, but it's also a fun time of fellowship.

There's just the Tuesday night Bible study as a midweek service. As well as Bible study, there's reading and prayer, and the pastor ministers on a more mature level for Christians. On Sunday he's aware that people are there who don't know the Lord at all.

Pastor Bernard says that if you take home what you get in a Sunday service, and you study it, go through the Bible, look up the Scriptures, apply them to yourself, pray about them, and apply them to your life, you don't need a Sunday evening service.

25

LEAVING LINWOOD

❧

Linwood would say: 'Oh, just because you've decided that *you* want to be religious, you think that everybody in the world has got to be religious with you.' And I said, 'No, Linwood, that's not what I think. I'm just talking to you about what I believe, and what I know is true.'

'Yeah, yeah, you know it's true, but I know God. Don't think that God can't talk to me. You think you're the only one that knows God . . .'

We were not speaking one another's language. The Assemblies of God church hadn't been able to help me, so God had had to pull me away from it. Now he also had to pull me away from Linwood.

❧

I went over to England in the spring of 1988 and while I was there I went to a Christian Convention in Brighton where the American evangelist John Wimber was preaching. A singer and good friend called Danny Owen was there, and introduced me to a girl called Bebe Russell and later her husband, Len. Bebe and I became friends immediately, and have been friends ever since. An odd thing happened on the last night of that convention. We were all standing up, praying and singing. I closed my eyes and I heard the Lord saying to me, 'Kneel down.' But I didn't. I thought Bebe and the others might think I was sort of showing off, trying to look more religious than they were. So I just stood there, with my eyes shut, singing and praying. When I opened my eyes – I was the only one still standing! Every single other person in that auditorium was down on their knees!

Because things were really not good at home, I decided to stay a couple of weeks in England with Bebe and her family in Catford. I went to her church at South Lee, and was ministered to there while I tried to get my head together.

One of the big troubles between Linwood and me at this time was that I had heard the Lord's call to ministry in music. I had been talking on the telephone with Milly, a friend of mine, and she told me that I shouldn't sing secular music any more. I said, 'There's nothing wrong with my music, and I've never sung about sex or drugs or anything like that. What's wrong with my music?'

She said, 'I don't know, Gloria. I just feel like you shouldn't be doing that.'

And these words came out of my mouth – I'll never forget them:

'Well, as long as my music is being used to draw people into places where drugs are available and they are encouraged to drink and dance beyond moral control, then my music is being used to condone things of the Enemy.'

And I heard what I said, and I said, 'I'll call you back.' I hung up, and I immediately got on my knees in prayer and said:

'Lord, is that how you feel about my music?'

And the Lord said, 'Yes.'

'So I can't do it any more? I'll clean up my lyrics, and I'll put a gospel song on every album . . .'

The Lord said, 'No.'

'OK . . . Then . . . I'll make sure that the record company allows me to put *half* gospel, and half secular.'

And the Lord said, 'No.'

'OK. Well, then I'll just have to stop singing altogether, except gospel music.'

And the Lord said, 'No.'

So I said, 'Well, what do you want me to do? I don't know what you want me to do. I'm not going to do *anything* until you let me know what you want.'

And the Lord said, 'Right.'

Linwood thought, 'She has gone! She has truly gone all the way crazy . . . She's pulled the rug out from under me, because I have stopped being a policeman. I gave all that up for her. I've spent all of my life savings on her in the hospital. I have married her and brought her to live in my home. I have wrapped myself up in her, her life has become my life. And now, she's just going to pull the rug out from under me. She just doesn't care about me, or anybody else, all she cares about is this stupid church and what the preacher's telling her. And the preacher and those people are telling her that she can't sing this music, and she's got to stop now, and she's just going to kill me . . .' He saw it all as advice, unnecessary and grossly damaging to our relationship and lives.

Linwood is an emotional man, and I was really stepping on his manhood. I was saying, in action if not in words, that I really didn't need him any more.

I didn't realize, and really, God knows, I'm so sorry, because I did not understand what I was doing to him as a man.

Linwood, although not a born again Christian, understands that I am the image of his glory. He does understand that a woman is representative of the man that she's with, because the man is to guide, guard and govern his woman, nurture her, and 'grow her up' in the ways of the world and the things of the Lord. And if he can't do that, then he feels inadequate as a man. And I was making him feel all that. And I didn't know it. I was feeling like a victim, but he was also the victim.

He was right in one thing – all I was interested in was what God wanted me to do. He didn't see it as that – he saw it as what the *church* wanted me to do. I honestly didn't know what God wanted me to do. The only thing I was sure about was that at that point God would have me do – nothing. Learn about him. Get rooted and grounded in my faith. Learn what he wanted me to do about my music.

Linwood was saying, 'I understand that you want to sing gospel music. That's fine!' But his idea was 'Spend a few dollars, do a gospel music album. You'll be happy, God will be happy, and then you can go on building your career with the *real* music.' I knew that wasn't the way it was supposed to go.

❧

My mother said to my brother one day, 'You know, Ralph, it's getting warmer outside. Why don't you take the lining out of your raincoat, and have it cleaned?'

So he left and he went to the cleaners. Weeks later it was raining, and my mother said, 'Why don't you wear your raincoat?'

He said, 'It's dirty.'

She said, 'No. I told you to get it cleaned a long time ago.' He'd only got the lining cleaned!

With the Lord, you need time to understand what he's saying. You have to develop a one to one personal relationship with him, where you've got to know his voice, and the way he deals with *you* as an individual. You may hear something and run off and do it, but if you haven't really understood what God was talking about, it can really hurt people, and make them feel scarred and betrayed.

I had stopped singing secular music, but I still believed God was calling me to a ministry in music. I started looking around for a record company that would record me singing gospel music. I found out about a record company in England. I contacted them while I was over in England and we arranged that I would do a big Christmas gospel concert. It was to be a Farewell Secular Music, Hello Gospel concert, the one recorded by the BBC for Radio 2.

I did not realize that the director of the music company was intending to book and manage me, and try to sidestep both Linwood and Malcolm Feld. I wouldn't have let that happen anyway, but I thought that he should be involved because, after all, neither Linwood nor Malcolm knew anything about gospel music or about ministering or anything. They needed help. I was to learn to my cost that he could have learned a great deal from Linwood.

He told me he had all sorts of well-known artists on his books, when all he actually had was a string of unknowns. I'm told he was desperate to get me on his books, and told the BBC that he was my agent, sidelining Malcolm Feld. He got all the money for the BBC contract, and caused me no end of trouble. So my first experience of Christian music management was fairly awful.

I did do the concert, although there were terrible fights over money. I really missed Linwood, whom I had hardly seen all that year. And I had a cold. The first part of the concert was all secular music, and the second part was all gospel music. During the first part I almost completely lost my voice but as soon as I began the first gospel song, almost miraculously my voice came back!

I was in England for a good part of 1988. Three weeks before the Hello Gospel Concert was due I had completed another series of engagements over there. I wanted to stay and spend more time with my friends at Bebe's church, because they had been really helping me. But I thought that Linwood would want me to come home. I talked to Bebe about it. [Bebe, by the way, is called that because the actress, Bebe Daniels, was her godmother.] She discussed it with some friends of hers, and called me and said, 'Well, we've discussed it and we've prayed about it, and we feel that the Lord is saying that you ought to stay here. Clare has a spare room in her home, and she wants you to come and stay with her.' So she brought Clare over to meet me in the hotel, but they had prayed on the way and heard the Lord saying that I was not to stay with Clare. I was to stay with a couple named Martin and Jenny Hemmings.

I didn't know Martin and Jenny Hemmings. Bebe said that she was finding it difficult to tell them that I should stay with them, because she knew that Martin and Jenny had moved into a new house and that it was an absolute wreck! They had ripped up the floors, torn all the wallpaper down and knocked down a wall of the kitchen to expand the living room. But they really felt that that was where the Lord wanted me to stay. So I said, 'Well, if that's where the Lord wants me to stay, perhaps he's not finished humbling me. I don't feel any check in my spirit about it, so I guess that's where I ought to stay.'

I called Linwood and he said it was fine by him for me to stay. Then I went to meet Martin and Jenny.

When they had bought the house, and sold their apartment, they had told the Lord it would be his house, and that they would always take in anyone he sent to them who needed refuge. But they were petrified at the thought of meeting 'the great Gloria Gaynor', a 'star', and wondered why ever I would want to stay with them!

They took me up this horrid staircase. Their own room was terrible, dust everywhere. But my room was lovely! Because theirs was to be a house of refuge, they had decided that the first room they'd get ready would be the guest room. It was freshly painted and all done up with Laura Ashley fabrics, with matching border round the ceiling – a really lovely little room.

Jenny was a teacher and Martin was in construction, so they were away all day. I could spend the whole day with the Lord. I'd get up in the morning and shower and get dressed. I would pull a chair over to the window and just sit there and look at the blue sky – there were blue skies even in London! I would just sit there and talk to the Lord. I would read the Bible and Christian literature. I would go downstairs, and play Christian music on the stereo, and sing to the Lord.

After two weeks I felt I should go home. I called Linwood and said I was coming home. He said, 'You've been there for two weeks! You had three weeks to come home, and now all of a sudden, after two weeks, with only one week left, now you want to come home?'

I said, 'Yeah, I want to come home.'

'Why?'

'Because I want to come home. I miss my home.'

'Well, who's going to pay for you to come all the way over here and go all the way back? Who's going to pay the fare?'

I said, 'I have my ticket to come home. The people who have booked my next engagement are going to pay my way back and home again.'

'You don't know that.'

'They are. They are. They don't even know that I've not gone back home. They expect me to be at home, to come from home. So they're going to pay my way over here and back.'

'They're not going to pay *nothing*. You don't know what you're talking about and I don't think you should come home now anyway.'

So I just hung up. And then I got to thinking, 'Has he got someone else.' I started to think that he had someone, or was carrying on an affair or whatever. I didn't know what was going on, but he seemed adamant that I should not come home. I really didn't want to run into anything that I didn't want to see, so I just hung up the telephone and went upstairs.

I went into my room and closed the door, and as I did it I heard the Lord saying, 'Go home. Now.'

I made my reservation that night. I didn't call Linwood again.

When I got home the doorman came out to the cab and loaded all my stuff on the trolley. I took the elevator, and rang the doorbell to our apartment, because I had left my keys behind when I left for England.

There was no answer.

When I had driven up I looked up and saw that the terrace doors were open, and the lights were on, so I thought Linwood was there. I started knocking. No answer. I rang, and I knocked, and I rang and I knocked. Then I went back downstairs and told the doorman to call the apartment and tell my husband that I was at the door. The doorman said, 'Oh, he just came in, so I told him that you were home.'

I thought he must have driven past the door, and gone into the garage to park, and then he'd be coming upstairs. So I went upstairs to meet him at the door. But still Linwood didn't come. I thought, 'Did he pass by my luggage and go into the house and close the door?' I rang the doorbell, and I didn't get any answer. Knocked, and no answer. Then I heard the telephone ring – once – so I thought he must have answered it. I thought, 'Ah! That's how to get his attention!' I went down to the next floor where there' s a public telephone, and called. The phone rang and rang and rang. No answer.

I thought, 'I guess when the doorman told him I was here, he left. He didn't want to see me.'

I went back down to the public telephone and called my niece, my eldest brother Ronald's daughter, Veronica, and asked her to come and get me. It took her a good forty-five minutes to get there, and still no Linwood. I put my things in her car and went to her house. I spent the night there. I called Linwood all evening long. No answer. And all day the next day, with no answer. The next day, finally, I got him.

I don't remember the conversation at all now, but I do remember that Linwood gave me no feeling that he wanted me to come home. He didn't ask me. He didn't say he'd come and get me. I thought, 'I'm not going home just to feel unwanted.' So I stayed with Veronica.

A week later I had to go back to England for a Christmas Concert and, after all I'd been through, it's not surprising I had a cold! Then I flew back to New Jersey, and went back to my niece's.

I called Linwood a few days later and asked him if I could come and get some things. He said, 'Yes, but I'm going out now.' This went on for six weeks. I kept on calling and he kept on making excuses to stop me from going round. Finally I said, 'Well, why don't you leave the keys with the doorman, and I'll let myself in when you're not there.'

And he said, 'I don't trust you.'

'Trust me? Not trust me to do what? Come into my own house?'

'I don't trust you. You have to come when I'm here.'

'OK, fine.' But I kept calling him and not getting any answer. So finally I said, 'Look, I've got to have my clothes. I've only got the clothes that I took to England with me. I can't go on like this.'

I got a locksmith to come with me and take the lock off the door. And I also went with moving-and-storage people, and a friend who was a policeman. He came in plain clothes so that Linwood wouldn't be embarrassed but I wanted a legal witness, in case he accused me of taking something, or we got into a row, or whatever. I just didn't understand why he wouldn't let me get my things.

The locksmith drilled through the metal door, making an almighty racket, and finally got the lock off the door.

The house looked like a dungeon. You could feel the gloom. Linwood had removed anything that would make you know that I had been there. He had removed all my trophies, my awards, my photos, my gold albums . . . he'd removed everything that would remind you that Gloria Gaynor had ever been there. I thought 'He's all but buried himself in this apartment.'

I told the removal people what was mine, and started moving

things out. I only took things that I knew Linwood wouldn't use – the Mixmaster from the kitchen and things like that.

And he was there! He was asleep, with the bedroom door closed. He could not hear. When he's in the bedroom with the door closed he can't hear. *I* hear. But he never heard anything. Later it was obvious that, on five or six of the times that I'd come round before, when I'd seen his car there but he hadn't answered the door, he'd been there. Asleep in the bedroom.

I woke him up and said, 'Linwood?'

He woke up with a start and yelled, 'How did you get in?'

So I said, 'Well, you know, I've called several times, and I've been trying to get in the apartment, and you never would let me in. You told me you didn't trust me. You wouldn't leave the keys downstairs for me … And I need my things.'

He kind of heard that, and didn't hear it. Linwood doesn't wake up very coherent at the best of times.

I gathered my clothes together and, while I was carrying them through, we met in the hallway between the bedroom and the living room. We looked into each other's eyes and I suppose he saw the love in my eyes, and I certainly saw the love in his. But I also saw the confusion. I said, 'I don't understand, either Linwood.' And I just passed by him, picked up the rest of my clothes, and left.

I went back to Veronica's, and stayed with her for several months. I had nowhere else to stay. It was very, very uncomfortable. My niece had a two-bedroomed apartment. She slept in one bedroom, her kids slept in the other bedroom, and I shared the same bedroom as my niece! It was a nice big room, but my niece was a young girl – she had boyfriends and stuff – and I was well and truly cramping her style! But she allowed me to stay there, knowing that I didn't have anywhere else to go.

❧

When it began to get really uncomfortable with Veronica, and I realized I would have to be moving on, I called Candi Staton and her husband, and asked if he would ask his mother, Mrs Marion Brown, if I could stay in her house. She lived alone and had three bedrooms and a finished basement. She'd talked, when I first met her, about how lonely she was. At the same time she said she didn't want anybody living in her house. So I thought, if he asked her, and she felt *more* that she didn't want anybody in her house than she felt lonely, then it would be easier for her to say 'No' to him. I didn't want to put her on the spot.

He called me and said, 'My mother says that she will not allow you to steal her blessing.' In other words, yes, I could stay with her, but I couldn't pay. It turned out that she was ill, and she really needed someone to be with her. She would have spells where she'd feel the room was spinning. Once or twice she'd had a turn in the car while she was driving, and become totally disorientated. So I began to drive her backwards and forwards to the doctor, and stayed with her in all for about three months. Then she began to feel better. She went back to work, and was able to drive again on her own. At the same time my niece, Veronica, had had to go into hospital, and didn't have anybody to take care of her when she came out.

She called me one day, collect. It was by now summer, the summer of 1989, and Veronica's children were away staying with their father, so she didn't have them to worry about. When she called, Mrs Brown wouldn't accept the charges. I came home one day and she said to me, 'Your niece just called collect. But I don't accept collect calls on my bill.'

I said, 'But I told you she was in hospital. She's in another city. I've no way of getting in touch with her to find out what she needs, whether she needs me to go there, whether she needs me to collect her. I've paid all my telephone bills here. You know I needed to hear from her. She calls collect, and you won't accept the charge?'

'I don't accept collect calls on my bill.'

'And you call yourself a Christian!' I thought.

I was livid. She had already started to get not so nice in other little things, and I prayed, Lord I hope I'm not being judgmental or ungrateful, but this is the last straw. I could drive her for hours, all day sometimes, to see her doctor and everything, but she hadn't let me borrow the car one day when I needed to go somewhere. I asked her, and she said no, so I never asked her again. I took the train.

This time again I took the train and the bus into New Jersey to see Veronica, and she was ready to leave the hospital. She didn't like what they were planning to do to her, and she was ready to get out of there, but she needed someone to take care of her.

The next morning Marion Brown said:

'I have to tell you something. I'm not used to people talking to me that way in my own home. I think it might be time for you to find yourself somewhere else to stay.'

I promised to leave that night. I went back to Veronica's, but I didn't know how long I would be able to stay there, or what would happen next.

Before I end this chapter, I want to give you Linwood's side of the story, so you'll see where he was coming from.

He never understood that I felt that he had locked me out. He never understood that, because he hadn't actually locked me out.

When the doorman said to me, 'I just saw him and told him that you'd just come in' well, he did see him, and did tell him that I had just come in, but Linwood thought he meant I had just come in *at the airport*. So he immediately drove off to the airport to meet me. And that was why my niece was able to come and get me and take me away and he still hadn't come back. When he arrived at the airport, and didn't see me, he went trying to find out about my flight. He'd parked and got a trolley, expecting to help with my luggage. He didn't know at that point that I didn't have my own key, so he thought that I was playing games to get him away from the house. He thought I had gone in and got what I wanted and left. If I was going to walk out on him like that, he wasn't going to beg for me to come back.

On the other hand I was thinking that if he had locked me out of the house and was avoiding me, I wasn't going to beg him to let me come back.

And that's why I believe that the Lord engineered it. So that we would be separated and grow. Because there was no way we were going to separate for good. We were going to just take each other's garbage. I really loved him. He really loved me. He thought I wasn't respecting him, and I thought that he wasn't respecting me. Neither one of us had the nerve to say, 'Get out!' or 'I'm leaving!' so we were never going to grow. We were never going to make any demands on one another, unless we did separate. I know that the Lord told me in no uncertain terms, 'Go home NOW.' And he knew what was going to happen. I would be alone and have time to stop and think. He wanted me to stop stumbling through my career, and trying to blunder my way into a music ministry, and doing everything my own way, and running ahead of him. If you run ahead of God, you end up there alone.

Linwood felt that I was trying to leave him. He thought that it was my decision to leave. He didn't know that I wanted to come back. I believe he thought I would come back, if he refused to give me my things. If I'd just said to him, 'I want to come home' then he would have been there.

But I didn't know all this. I thought, 'This man has lost it!'

Some friends did say to me, 'You know, this man is just sitting waiting for you to come back. He's not doing anything.'

A friend of his who lives in our building said that he'd go and see him and say, 'Come on, man, let's go out' and he would tell him, 'No, man. I miss my woman, man. I miss my woman.' Linwood just wouldn't do anything, he wouldn't go anywhere, not for Christmas, not for Thanksgiving.

I don't think that either of us doubted our love for the other during that whole year.

26

GETTING BACK

By September 1989 Linwood and I were talking once in a while on the telephone. We were friendly, but we didn't discuss getting back together, and we didn't talk about our careers. I was handling my own affairs – and messing up royally! But I had managed, with Malcolm's help, to set up my first ever all gospel tour in the UK, for November and December.

Meanwhile, I had gone back to stay with Veronica for the second time, and while I was there a girlfriend, Carol Williams, called who was getting married. We'd been friends for a long time, so of course she knew Linwood and me as a couple. She said, 'I want to invite Linwood. Do you mind if I send him one invitation for the two of you, so that you and he could come together?'

I said, 'I don't mind, if he doesn't mind.'

Carol sent him the invitation and he called me and asked if I would mind going with him. So we went to her wedding. I went the night before, to help her and to go to the wedding eve dinner. She realized she wasn't going to have time the next morning, her wedding morning, to go and get the minister, and asked me if Linwood would mind bringing the minister with him. I said, 'Honey, I don't know. You're going to have to ask Linwood yourself.' Usually he was not very accommodating. He wouldn't go out of his way to do anything for anybody. She called him and he said, 'Yeah!' I thought, 'He's changed! He has really changed!' He quite happily went to pick the minister up that morning. And was on time! Although, when I saw the minister, I wasn't quite so pleased about it, because she was beautiful!

The wedding was held in a beautiful banqueting hall with a chapel, and it was wonderful. Linwood and I spent the whole time together. We danced, and looked lovingly and longingly into each other's eyes. It was all very romantic.

9 October, a month later, was our tenth wedding anniversary, but I had blocked it out of my mind. I didn't want to be miserable and depressed because we weren't together. So when Linwood called and asked me if I'd like to have dinner with him at the house on our anniversary, I said, 'When is our anniversary?' He was so insulted! I'd always been the one before who'd had to remind him.

We had a lovely dinner together. He cooked a real Southern meal – fried chicken and potato salad and green beans cooked with some kind of smoked meat, and corn bread and sweet potato pie. Wow! Linwood, whom I'd never seen cook anything in his life before. And it was delicious!

We washed up together, and then sat and talked. I said, 'Now, Linwood, this is purely hypothetical. Purely hypothetical. But if we got back together, would you consider counselling?'

And he said, 'Let's put it like this, I *wouldn't* consider getting back together *without* counselling.'

I nearly fell off my chair. He was the kind of man who would always say, 'I don't need anybody to tell me how to handle my wife.' I thought, 'He's really changed!' I suggested that we go to my pastor. But he said, 'I don't want to go to no preacher. I don't want anybody preaching at me . . .' I said, 'Linwood. We don't have the money any more to go to a commercial, secular counsellor. So let's go to Pastor Bernard. He's free. He' s not going to tell us anything wrong, because he's a good, honest, straight up man. But if you don't like him, then we won't go back.'

So we went. Pastor Bernard was absolutely wonderful. We set up an appointment to go again and on that occasion Linwood opened up so much to him I was amazed and nearly started crying. He said, 'I'm a sentimental sort of man, Pastor.'

Pastor Bernard said, 'Do you have a problem with that?'

Linwood said in his gruff, macho voice: 'Nah. I don't have a problem with that. I'm just a sentimental man. That's it.'

After the second meeting the pastor said, 'Call me when you both feel ready to come back.' I wish now that I'd said 'No, let's set up the next meeting right now.' This was now the end of October and I was going off to the UK on my first ever gospel tour, and Linwood was coming with me. It was the first time we'd been together for over a year, and of course we travelled as man and wife.

We were communicating, we had had reconciliation, but I didn't realize that we still didn't have a real restoration of our trust in each other. I didn't realize the difference between reconciliation and restoration, or that you needed both before you should really get back together. I did say to him, 'Linwood, I want us to finish counselling with Pastor Bernard before we get back together, because I'm afraid that if we don't, it's going to end up the same way. I want us to set up some ground rules, and commit to keeping them.'

He agreed, but we didn't. The gospel tour took us off. We spent November and December in England, including Christmas with Bebe and her family in Catford. When we came back in January, I went back to my niece's, got my things and went home.

❖

We started off wonderfully! He was cooking, he was helping me in the house, vacuuming the floors, taking out the laundry, taking out the trash, and shopping, and doing all the things I'd always wished he'd done!

The cooking quickly stopped. The shopping quickly stopped. Well, he still does a little. If I call him and ask him to stop on the way home and bring something he will, which he never would before. He's ever so much more considerate and thoughtful than he was before.

We didn't get rid of our grievances straight away. Actually, it was to take the next three years. I was resenting a lot, unable to really trust Linwood because of the things that had happened. I did believe that he was through with drugs, and he'd nearly stopped drinking. He never was a big drinker anyway. He'd stopped partying all night, but he would still spend some nights out. He'd come home as if he'd just gone out to the post office or something. After he'd done it a few times, I went to Pastor Bernard and told him. He said, 'Well, you know he's testing you. Trust has been broken, and now you'll have to make a decision, and do something about it.'

So I told him it was unacceptable behaviour and I wasn't going to have it. He continued to do it anyway.

Things went rapidly downhill again. He still felt that I wasn't trusting him. I suspect he was also a little bit jealous of the relationship between me and Pastor Bernard, not understanding that it's like a counsellor/student, wise uncle/niece type relationship. Plus I was back to tithing, giving this preacher all his money, as far as he was concerned.

He'd got me back to work. Immediately we were reconciled I was back working, because he's an excellent manager. Pastor Bernard explained to me: 'When you left him, you took away his credibility from the people that worked with you. You broke up, but still they'd want to know: why is he not managing you any more? You took away his credibility.' When they don't have the facts, people all too often imagine the worst.

That was restored when we got back together and started working together again. Money was coming in, so things were better financially. But I was tithing, and he didn't like that at all.

We really couldn't get it together. I thought there was a lot still wrong with Linwood, but I had to learn that I had a lot of growing and changing to do myself. And because the days were strained, the nights weren't fantastic either.

27

UNDER NEW MANAGEMENT

One day someone ministered to me, just walked up to me out of the blue. They didn't know what I did, didn't know I was a singer. They said to me 'No, he will not manage you. "No man will share my glory."'

At first I thought they were talking about the guy from Ears and Eyes in England. But after Linwood and I got back together, and were having such problems, I decided they must have been talking about him.

So I told Pastor Bernard. And he said, 'Well, is he honest?'

I said, 'Yeah.'

'Is he capable?'

I said, 'Yeah.'

'Is he conscientious?'

I said, 'Yeah!'

'So why would the Lord say that he wasn't to manage you?'

But a lot of well-meaning Christian friends kept saying to me, 'Blessed is the man that walketh not in the council of the ungodly.' That was the Scripture that they used to back up their belief that Linwood was not to manage me. Several people told me that. I was thinking, 'But how can I do that? How can I not let him manage me? How? How?' He was going to think that I was pulling the rug from under him again, and that I did not really care about him. Would God really ask me to do that? I also thought: 'We've got this contract. I don't have any money to get a lawyer. It's really going to be so difficult.'

So many things were happening. Scriptures kept coming to me.

I was talking about it with somebody, and I said, 'But he's done so much for me. How can I do this to him? How can God ask me to do that to him?'

Then I got what I thought was a vision, of myself leaning over a crib. There was a baby. It was my baby. And the doctor was there with a needle full of some kind of medicine. The baby was sick, and I would not let the doctor give the baby the medicine, because the needle was going to hurt.

I felt the Lord saying to me: 'You're trying to protect him, as if you think I can't.' I thought, 'Well, if this is what God wants me to do, then God will supply his needs. He'll give him another way. Maybe he needs to be down and out before he'll hear from the Lord, and maybe I'm standing in the way.'

Then I was talking to somebody about it, and I said, 'But he's done so much for me.'

And they said, 'And the Lord is saying: "And what have I done for you?"' I didn't know what to do.

I thought, 'Before I accepted Christ as my Saviour, I was putting Linwood before God. I was doing things that I knew I had no business doing. I was doing things that I knew – even before I knew Christ – that God did not want me to do. But in order to hang on to Linwood, I would go against God. I can't do that any more.'

I had already faced this with tithing. I insisted that I was going to tithe, whether he liked it or not. In that way I had made my decision not to put Linwood before God. And now I thought God was testing me again, and I was not going to fail.

I wrote Linwood a letter telling him how and why he could no longer be my manager, that I was going to take our contract to a lawyer and have it broken.

It was 1990, the day before New Year's Eve, and I asked the Lord for a sign as to whether or not I should wait until after New Year to give him this letter. The night before I folded up a wet cloth and left it in the bathroom, and I said to the Lord, 'If this cloth is completely dry in the morning, then I'll know that you want me to tell him right away.' I woke up in the morning, and the cloth was bone dry. But then I thought, 'Oh, it's just dried up overnight.' So I put the same cloth, that was dry, and said, 'If it's wet in the morning, then I'll know.' I woke up the next day – it was sopping wet.

So on New Year's Day I gave him the letter. He looked at me in total disgust and just threw the letter aside as if he was going to ignore it.

I remembered another friend of mine, who had been under contract with her husband and, when they broke up, she hadn't been able to break her contract. She went on working anyway, without him, and never heard from him again. I thought that that was the way God was going to work it for me.

Months went by. I didn't know what to do. I was still working with him and doing engagements, and still hearing from my friends that the only reason I wasn't taking any action was because I was scared, and that God would help me if I would just go ahead and do it. I said, 'But nobody's telling me *how* to do it.'

'Pray to God for a good lawyer, and the lawyer will tell you what to do to get out of this contract ... God wants you to get out of this contract because you cannot keep working with him ... You're concerned about your marriage and putting your marriage before God ... Aagh! They're telling me all this stuff, and I still don't know what to do.

Pastor Bernard's words began to ring in my ears: 'Why would God tell you that he can't manage you?' It was not as if Linwood was telling me to do anything that was not of the Lord. Had I *tried* to do more gospel music, to see what he would say about it? Linwood had been saying, 'Sure, you can do a gospel album. I'll find you somebody to do a gospel album.'

In spite of this, I hardened my heart. I had given him fair warning, and I went to a lawyer. He told me the contract was iron-clad. Linwood had everything for himself, and had promised me nothing. All it said was that he would do his best. Whatever that might mean.

I said, 'Well I really honestly feel that he has been doing his best. And I felt like that was guarantee enough, because the more he did for me, the more would be done for him.'

Then one day Linwood said to me, 'I'm going to find somebody to buy out your contract. You want another manager? Fine. I'll find somebody to buy out your contract. And I hope you do well.'

Every now and then, every six months or so, I'd ask him, 'Did you find somebody?'

✿

In 1992 Linwood asked me for a divorce. I went into the kitchen and sat down and he said, 'I want a divorce.'

I said, 'You've got it!'

And he said, 'Contrary to what you think, we *will* be working together. Now this divorce can be nice and easy, or it can be nasty. It's up to you.'

I said, 'No problem.' I went into the office and I called Pastor Bernard and told him that Linwood had asked for a divorce.

He said, 'Really? How do you feel about it?'

I thought for a second and then I said: 'Free at last! Free at last! Thank God Almighty I'm free at last!' Then I laughed. I said, 'You know, Pastor Bernard, I don't know how I'll feel about this in a couple of weeks, but that's how I feel right now.'

I was sick of it. Sick of the turmoil. He said we'd be working together but I knew that if we weren't living together, Linwood wouldn't want to work with me, so the contract would be broken and God would have his way.

Pastor Bernard found me another lawyer. I told him about the divorce and showed him the contract. He said the same thing about the contract – it was ironclad. But he said, 'Perhaps if you offer him something more than what he's getting in this contract, then you could substitute it – tear up this contract and substitute it with another one.' They weren't music lawyers, and it was stupid of me really to have talked to them about it. Pastor Bernard had sent me to them for the divorce, but they wanted to do the two things together. They wanted to go to the judge and say that the only reason I had signed the contract originally was because he was my husband, or was just about to become my husband, and that was part and parcel of the marriage. Now that the marriage was over, the contract was over. Perhaps they'd go for that. If not, then because of my name, I could get other artists to sign up with us to form a management company. Linwood would still be head of the management company, but I would assign someone else to attend to my particular needs.

At first I thought this was great, because then he would not only be getting a percentage of what I made, he'd also be getting a percentage of all these other artists. And he'd be busy, and earning money, so it would not be like I was giving him anything. Then I thought, if I did that, Linwood would want to manage secular artists, not gospel singers, and my name would be attached to any garbage they might record. I didn't want that. So we were talking it back and forth.

A couple of weeks later Linwood came to me and said he didn't want a divorce. I said, 'What?'

He said, 'Do you know why I asked you for a divorce? Because I thought you were taking birth control pills.'

From 1990 I had been getting really heavy-duty pains in my back and found that once again I had fibroids. I'd already had them removed in 1975. Now they were getting worse and worse, and every doctor I went to told me that I would have to have a hysterectomy. But I didn't want one, not only because I was still hoping to have children one day, even at my age, but also because I believe that if your womb and your ovaries are no longer useful once you are past childbearing age, God would have made them shrivel up or something, and he didn't. They must be doing something else for you, and I wanted to keep everything that God gave me.

Finally I said, 'OK, I'll have the hysterectomy.' But I said to the Lord, 'I know you'll do something. I've been praying to you about this, about not having a hysterectomy. I'll just go ahead. Do whatever you're going to do.'

I told my friend, Carol Williams, that I was very reluctantly going to have a hysterectomy, and she said she had a book she wanted me to read, called *The Castrated Woman*. I assumed that the book would make me more comfortable with my hysterectomy.

As I was now comfortable with the idea that I was going to do it, if God was going to let me, I didn't feel I needed to read the book. So I put it to one side, and thought I'd get around to it sooner or later.

The doctor said my blood count was too low to proceed and that I should go away for a month and take iron tablets, and then come back for the operation. I had to go to Italy to make a recording, and I took the book with me. When I had some free time I started reading this book. In retrospect, I can just hear the Lord saying, 'You've been praying for help – read the book, stupid!'

I was sitting in the studio one day, and I got to the back of the book, and I saw a section about a woman gynaecologist who had written a book called *No More Hysterectomies*. She believed that fibroids are never a reason for having a hysterectomy.

Well I put the book down immediately, picked up the telephone to Linwood and asked him to find this woman. I read the section to him. So he found her. Her name was Dr Hufnagle. I called her, told her the whole story, and she said, 'Don't worry, honey, we'll take care of you.'

I made an appointment to go and see her.

I then got Linwood's sister Denise, our secretary, to ring the doctor who was going to perform the hysterectomy to say that I was going to get a second opinion, and that I'd get back to him. Before she could finish telling him he slammed the telephone down on her. He was extraordinarily angry. It was all the more reason for my not wanting to ever go back to him again.

So I went out to Dr Hufnagle and she examined me and told me she could take care of it and would not have to remove my plumbing! I had more than twenty fibroids removed. The mass was the size of a seven-month-old foetus. She filmed the operation, removing all these fibroids, and gave me a video of it!

I really don't understand why so many women agree to have hysterectomies. No way would a man have that. A man equates his manhood with his reproductive system.

Anyway, Linwood thought that now he'd got me all well and now I was secretly protecting myself from somebody else. I must be having an affair. He'd seen these tiny little pills that he thought were birth control pills. He'd asked some stupid manfriend of his, who'd said, 'Yep. That's what they are – birth control pills.' They were *iron* tablets. When he'd found out, he was satisfied and no longer wanted a divorce. I'm so insecure, and, well, yeah, I loved him. I've always loved him. But I didn't even have the nerve to say, 'Oh, you're just "on again, off again". I'm supposed to hop into the marriage, out of the marriage when you snap your fingers, whenever you say, and I have nothing to say about it.' That's what I was thinking, and feeling. But I just said, 'All right. OK.'

I went back to the lawyers and told them that I no longer wanted a divorce, but I allowed them to keep on with the contract thing.

When Linwood found out, he was livid. Positively livid.

So I kept trying to come up with ways of getting out of this contract, but without letting Linwood down. I still wanted the marriage. It just wasn't happening. It wasn't working out. It had come to a kind of stalemate. Nothing I came up with was good enough. It was not what Linwood was going to accept.

I kept getting bills, because every time you sit down with lawyers they charge you for it, but we weren't coming to any conclusions. So I stopped going to them. This thing still came between us, because Linwood knew about it. Not only that, he was still every now and then staying out at night. He went out one night and stayed away for three nights. I thought, 'That's it. Forget it. I'm alone anyway. If he's going to do this, I'm alone anyway. So why bother?'

Then I remembered what Pastor Bernard had said about it being a test, and that it was up to me to say something.

So I said, 'I don't know if this will mean anything to you. As a friend of ours once said, "A warning is a blessing. It's a gift." This relationship, this marriage, can very easily deteriorate back to what it was in 1989 if you insist on staying out all night.' And I got up and walked away.

The next morning he said, 'You know, I've thought about what you said!' and I said, 'Good.' And nothing else was ever said about it. He's never stayed out again all night, except to stay at his mother's, or with his brother. But then he'd always make sure he'd call me and let me know where he was.

I never thought I was going to divorce Linwood.

Even when he asked me for a divorce, I never thought I was going to divorce him. And even when I thought maybe we would go through with the divorce, I would say, 'People get remarried all the time.' A divorce was only ever going to be on paper. It was never going to be in our hearts.

And that's the way he was feeling about it.

I think we both felt when we married we committed to each other for life. This was just something we had to go through. Once it was over, things would be fine. We were in the dark groping for each other, and not knowing how to find our way. It's like saying 'I smell you. I feel you. But I don't see you and I can't get to you. But I know you are there for me. And I'm here.'

Pastor Bernard gave us the first direction. I went to counselling with him again. I told him what was happening because I was still in a sort of turmoil. This was 1992. He said:

'I hear the Lord telling me to tell you to find, learn and prepare to minister to the congregation a song called "Changed".' The song's a very simple song, it says, 'A change has come over me. He saved my life and set me free. He washed away all my sins . . .' and then it tells all the ways that I've been changed.

I found the song, played it and . . . I hated it! Well I liked the lyrics but hated the melody and the arrangement – the whole way the song was done. At church the band knew and loved it, as did the choir. The choir had to sing the song with me, and after the first two very short verses it was as much the choir as me singing. It didn't bother me, but I just didn't like it. Also in order to be really effective it called for somebody that had a really high range. I had cysts on my vocal chords removed and ever since then my range has never been the same. So I wasn't able to perform it like I wanted to.

But God is so clever. Because he knew I wasn't going to like this song, which meant that I could not 'perform' the song, I had to *minister* it. I had to be walking in what the song was saying.

I had not been walking in the changes the Lord was making in me, because I was afraid to. But perfect love casts out all fear. And Christ should bring confidence into your life as to who you are. Your sufficiency and your expectancy must only be in Christ. These are the things that the Lord brought to me while I was learning this song.

I really began to grow. I began to become confident about

myself. God had wiped away the loneliness. So why was I insecure? There shouldn't have been any insecurity. It was all a lie that the Enemy had sold me and I had bought part and parcel. I was walking in that, instead of walking in the truth of who I had become in Christ, or walking in the changes that God had made in me.

I began to recognize that I had every reason to be confident. And, as a matter of fact, I *was* confident. And if Linwood left me – who cares? Of course I loved him. Of course I wanted him ... but I wasn't desperate any more. If he wasn't going to allow me to walk in truth, he would have to leave me.

So I began to walk in truth. And do you know what happened? Linwood's respect for me grew – so much that I could not believe it! He saw the girl that he first fell in love with. He saw the girl that he fell in love with because she was self-sufficient and she was confident, and she had a lot going for her.

When all of that had taken a back seat because of my need for him in my life, then his level of respect had dropped, and he had begun to act the way he did. If you lie down on the floor, people are going to think that you think you're a carpet, and walk on you!

I had never understood it before. Also, until I found the Lord, there was no confidence. Everything that I had confidence in was temporal, wavering, dying . . . But there was no reason for any of that any more.

❀

In the past two years, as I've walked in truth, and grown and been able to grasp and implement in my life more and more the principles and precepts the Bible teaches, Linwood is gaining more confidence in me, more respect and more love for me.

So now, in truth, Linwood is not managing me. I'm under new management – God is managing me, through Linwood.

28

CHANGED

Malcolm Feld, my agent in England, asked me one day if I thought I'd changed since becoming a Christian, and I said, 'Yes.'

He said, 'Well, let me tell you that you have changed very much. In fact you've made a 180-degree turnaround. Before you were a Christian, Gina used to hate it when we knew you were coming over. She asked me never to make her be around when you were here. You were sarcastic, selfish, self-centred, demanding and thoughtless. But now we both love you. We love having you in our home. You are thoughtful, generous, kind and there's nothing that we wouldn't do for you.'

I said, 'Malcolm, I must admit, it's not me, but Christ in me. It's what he has done for me. Only Christ can change the heart of an individual.'

And Malcolm said, 'Well, I want to tell you – he's doing a great job!'

Most people have many acquaintances, and very few real friends in life, and I've never been any different, except that I've been blessed since becoming a Christian with four *best* friends! I'm not sure if geography has anything to do with it, but they all live nearly 3000 miles apart. There's one in Los Angeles, one in New York, one in New Jersey, close by, and one in England.

The one I've known longest is Florence Dixon, nicknamed Fippy. I've already told you a little bit about her. Fippy lives in Los Angeles. I met her in New York, through my manager. Although she soon moved away to Los Angeles, we became reacquainted in 1975 when I went out to LA to appear on the 'American Bandstand' television show, performing 'Never Can Say Goodbye', which was my hit song at that time. It was then that we really connected and knew that we would become lifelong friends. Fippy was already a born-again Christian, the only one I knew in fact. Sometimes Fippy was the only person in the world I felt I could confide in.

Sondra, my second best friend, is also my sister-in-law, Sondra Simon Robinson, once of Simon Said. She lives in New York. She's been sister, friend, companion, pal, and mutual confidante, like Fippy, and also room-mate, travelling companion, and, of course, backing singer! She too has been born again now. We've seen much of the world together, and been through innumerable happy and sad experiences, as friends, as professional colleagues, and as members of the same family.

My third best friend is Darcel Moreno. She lives very near us in New Jersey, and I met her at Gospel Tabernacle Church there. Although Darcel is quite a bit younger than I am, she is a Christian and therefore, through the wisdom of God, we often reverse back and forth the roles of mother and daughter, coun-selling one another and giving one another guidance. Her natural maturity, and the fact that we have Christ, among many other things, in common, makes our ages irrelevant. That all sounds a bit solemn. Believe me, when Darcel is around, neither of us ever stops talking and laughing. We're the kind of friends who will talk on the phone for an hour, then decide to hang up and visit each other!

I've mentioned the young British singer named Danny Owen, who I met through a client of my agent, Malcolm Feld in 1988. Danny and his wife Yvonne invited me to their home. I enjoyed their company very much and, as I was over working in England quite a bit that year, I was soon spending a couple of days with them whenever I could. We became really good friends.

Not long after, at the John Wimber Conference, Danny intro-duced me to Bebe Russell who I've spoken about frequently in this book. She was to become my fourth very best friend. At that time Bebe and her family lived in Catford, near London, and I frequently used to stay with them, and as time went on our friend-ship just began to grow and grow. Now the Russells have moved out into Essex, and live not far from Danny and Yvonne, so the two families and I get to spend quite a bit of time all together. I've spent many memorable hours in their two homes, including several Christmases. What Fippy, Sondra, Darcel and Bebe have in common is that they are all very loving, caring people. They all have children whom I love dearly. They all have a personal relation-ship with the Lord Jesus, as I do. They all love me, and I love all of them. They are as much 'family' to me as the children my mother bore. We've laughed, cried and prayed together. We've experienced and shared so much with each other, that time and distance cannot separate us, and because we all have Christ, death won't either.

My church in Brooklyn, the Christian Life Centre, has over 5,000 people, but the choir only consists of 45 people. You might expect a church that size to have a much bigger choir, but Pastor Bernard sees the choir as a ministry. I believe, we both believe, that one of the reasons why the Church hasn't got a larger population in the world than it does is because we have ignored the music ministry.

In the Bible, the musicians were always the first to go out before battle. Music prepares the heart to receive the Word. In most churches music isn't *ministered,* it's just sung to be enjoyed. The anointing of the Lord is not a part of it, and therefore the heart is not prepared to hear the Word from God. Very often there is no Word coming forth anyway. Christians don't need to be preached at, they need to be taught, and there aren't all that many teachers. You get a lot of preachers who aren't teachers. Their people are baby Christians, and remain babies. They don't mature and learn how to occupy territory for Christ until His Return – which has been our call.

Pastor Bernard says that 'we preach separation, and we practise segregation'. We need to be separate from the world, but we mustn't be segregated. You must mingle with people and be where they are, so they can see that we have what they need, without condemning them for not having it. Sadly some Christians do condemn – when it's only through grace that any of us has it. It's only by the grace of God any of us is saved. We're not better than anybody else, and the Bible says, 'If God cut off the Jews, who were the vine, the original vine, and grafted you in – you be careful! Don't think he's not going to cut you off, if you forget who you are or who he is.' We all need to be very, very careful.

Ministering that song 'Changed' made me see a lot of things differently. It confirmed what the Lord told me when he released me to go back to my career in 1990: 'As long as your music is created and performed for my glory, and is in keeping with the holy life that I call you to live and advocate, your music is not secular – it is sanctified.' I have realized that doing only gospel music was not what the Lord was calling me to do. He wants me to minister to the world. In order to do that, to minister to a non-spiritual person's spirit, one must get past the flesh. I have to continue singing secular music, interspersing it with gospel music.

That's my directive for now. Whether the Lord will call me to do only gospel music one day, I don't know. I do know that I will be doing more and more gospel. The gospel will become the major part of what I'm doing at some point, which will launch me into a real ministry. Right now I'm kind of hanging out on the fringes of a ministry. It's not my time yet.

One day the Lord will tell me my time has come, and I will minister Christ to a world that was opened up to me by the song 'I Will Survive'.

29

SOUL SURVIVOR

❖

So, you see, I have survived! And I will survive.

Of course I have some regrets about my life. I think there was an easier way to get to where I am now, and I wish I had taken it. I'm not going to moan about it but I wish I had made better choices. I don't believe people who say they have no regrets. I believe there's always an easier way to get to where you end up as an adult.

I don't think that you really have to trudge through the mud. You know what I'm saying? If you're going to wash your clothes, they don't have to be filthy. But if you've gone by the worst way, and don't use that to keep someone else from going through doing the same, then your mistakes have really served no purpose. So I really do hope to lead someone away from the pitfalls. Even if I didn't learn by my mistakes, I hope somebody does!

If any young person is reading this book who is lonely and unsure of themselves as I was, I would say, 'Find yourself a good church and get some good, clean friends!' Finding the church that is right for you isn't always that easy, as I discovered. But keep persevering, trying to let God lead you.

Being 'in' is not all it's cracked up to be. If you want to grow and learn about yourself and what it takes to make you who you want to be, then you need to have a good example. You don't want to follow the crowd, tagging along with wild young people who have had no real experience of life. They may be your friends, but don't copy them. Learn from people who have been there.

I would have to say to all parents that your children really do need to be encouraged, not scolded and criticized. They need to be given a strong sense of self-worth, a good sense of identity, and need to be accepted for who they are, trusted, praised and appreciated. They should be given choices, and helped to make the right decisions not only by words, but by good example.

Parents need to be heroes. If they don't give love, attention and instruction from God's word to their children, the children often spend the rest of their lives trying to please them. Even after the parents are dead, they'll still be trying to please them instead of God.

I don't grieve any more that Linwood and I don't have children. I don't feel any real grief, but I feel a loss. I longed to have children, and to show my mother what a great mother I was! I settled that I was OK without children about six or seven years ago.

I don't think Linwood was ever really bothered about it. He's had two children from previous relationships, but one we never see now. The other, Nahdir, is grown-up, and I love her like my own daughter. She has a daughter of her own, our granddaughter, three-year-old Jerlaine, whom we both love dearly. She's smart as a whip, and wraps us both round her little finger. She's such a little doll. So I do have a granddaughter. She calls me and says, 'Ganma, Mummy won't let me have the telephone.'

I say, 'Yes, but you see, honey, the telephone is not a toy.'

I'm glad to be free. If I'd had children when I wanted to, I guess I'd be free by now, but I don't really, really want to have children now. If I did get pregnant now, I'd be ecstatic. I'd be praying day and night that the baby and I would stay healthy, and that I'd give birth to a baby with ten fingers and ten toes. And I always wanted lots of children. A big family. I wanted a little girl, and five or six older brothers for my little girl, like I had. I'd have made sure they weren't useless, like my brothers were! Gee, they were useless! (I say that most affectionately!)

We've got thirty-nine nephews and nieces last time I counted, so I've never been short of children to give affection to. My sister Irma has three children, Simone, Hassanah and Max. Irma was pregnant with Max, and she came over to the house to spend the weekend with us. We all went out to dinner and Linwood said to her, 'Why don't you name the baby after me?' and she said 'OK.'

'I'm serious.'

'I'm serious too! Tom doesn't like his name – he hates anybody to call him Uncle Tom! So he won't mind. I'll name him after you. We'll name him Linwood Maxwell.'

And he said, 'Oh! Then wouldn't it be great if he could be born this month, because it might be on my birthday?'

She said, 'There ain't no way he's going to be born this month, because I'm only six months pregnant. Forget it!'

Then while we were still at the restaurant, her stomach started hurting, and she was miserable, so we said, 'OK, let's get some doggy bags and go on back to the house.' So we went home. She went to the bathroom and said that she was spotting blood.

We called Tom to come and take her home and get her to her doctor. She had the baby on the way! She started having contractions, he took her to the hospital, and she had little Max on 11 April, a week before Linwood's birthday. So he was named Linwood Maxwell. We call him Max, but he calls himself Linwood. He wants to be called Linwood. Everybody calls him Max, and every time he corrects you, and says 'Linwood'. But nobody wants to call him Linwood. He's a sweet kid, and he wraps his uncle round his little finger. Linwood took him as his godson.

Linwood still has his publishing company. He has a couple of writers under contract. I'm still under contract as a writer, and he's still managing me. For the most part our friends are still separate. He keeps his friends away from me. I always know who he'll like of my friends and, when I insist that he meets somebody, he always likes them. He kicks and screams and says he doesn't want to be bothered and all of that, but they always instantly love him, and he always likes them, so we do have a few friends in common. Linwood is one of those naturally attractive people that people are always drawn to, especially kids. He's very much a home body now. He loves his home, and we get along just fine.

When I met Linwood, I was looking for a man who was domineering, smart. I wanted him to be guide, guard and governor of my life. That is what a father and a husband ought to be. The problem is that neither can do their job properly unless he has had it in his own life from the ultimate guide, guard and governor, Christ.

Whenever I'm in LA staying with my best friend, Fippy, I go to the Shabach Christian Fellowship where there is a wonderful minister, Pastor Johnson, who has ministered to me and helped me through many problems. I've been to Pastor Johnson's church many, many times. She is just a gifted and anointed minister, and has a house-guest, a lawyer whose name is Margaret. I will never forget what Margaret said to me one time, and I have repeated this to many other women and been blessed by it. She said to me:

'You know, Gloria, you need to stop relying on your husband to do things for you that he isn't capable of doing. It isn't that he doesn't love you, it's just that there are certain things that he's incapable of doing. You need to learn that your dependency, and sufficiency, should only be in Christ.'

That has relieved me from putting pressure on my husband. It has eased up the tension in our relationship, and been a great blessing. I must give Linwood credit for recognizing that, as his wife, I am representative of the man he is. He taught me, groomed me, appreciated me. He encourages me, protects me, leads me, guides me and loves me, and is doing a great job. God blesses me with and through Linwood.

I was never satisfied with the way we got married, though, and we will have to renew our vows one day. I say we'll do it when Linwood is born again, and we'll have a new creation marriage.

For a few years I had my time in the wilderness. In order to grow spiritually, I needed to spend some time away from my professional career, which made things difficult financially. But it was absolutely necessary. I have no anxiety about the future. Linwood's going to be saved, and it's going to be wonderful! I'm not expecting things to be perfect, but there will be easier communication. At the moment it's still difficult for me to communicate spiritual things to him.

It's funny, because when I was praying about Linwood's salvation, and really praying about how Linwood felt about me and my 'religion', the Lord said, 'You're bringing the light to him. It's like when you wake someone up out of the dark, out of a deep sleep, and you just turn on the light. The light is very harsh and very irritating, and they get very irritated about it. But after awhile they get used to the light, and like having it on. And that's what will happen in your relationship.'

And that is what is happening. Linwood has already started to share some Christian things with me. For instance, we 'adopted' two children as part of a UNICEF scheme that I wanted to join. We did that together.

The Lord also told me that when you minister to people, it's like when people are sitting in a dark room and you open the door. Those who are furthest away from the door will take the longest period of time to see, get used to, and enjoy the light. Those two things have been very helpful to me in ministering to Linwood.

He's now got to the point where he believes me when I tell him things that have happened in my life, little miracles, and things that the Lord has given me. He's got kind of used to the light!

When I wanted to rerecord 'I Will Survive' for the *Gloria Gaynor '90* album that I recorded in Italy, that eventually went gold, I wanted to change some of the words to reflect my new Christian beliefs. I wanted to call Freddy Perren and ask him if I could do it, because you have to have permission. So I was praying, 'Lord, please give me favour with these people. I really don't want to go through any changes with them . . .' I'd had a little difficulty with them in the past, when they had seemed to me to be quite unsympathetic and difficult to deal with.

Linwood didn't want to call them, so I said I would. When we were in the studio in Italy, getting ready to do it, I was trusting God to work it out for me. Linwood got Freddy Perren's in L.A. on the telephone, and called me, 'Gloria, do you want to speak to them?'

I came over and said, 'Hi, Christine! How you doing?'

'Hi, Gloria! Freddy's on the other line. I understand that you want to change some of the words to "I Will Survive"?'

'Yes, I do. I hope that's not a problem for you . . .'

I told her the change I wanted to make. She said, 'Oh, honey! When I heard that you were born again, we were so excited! Praise the Lord! Glory to God!'

They were born again too! I said to the Lord, 'God, when you fix it, you really fix it, don't you?'

Only the Lord could give me strength
not to fall apart
Though I tried hard to mend the pieces
of my broken heart.
And I spent oh! so many nights
just feeling sorry for myself.
I used to cry
but now I hold my head up high!
And you see me
somebody new
I'm not that chained up little person
still in love with you.
And so you felt like dropping in
And just expect me to be free?
Well now I'm saving all my loving
for Someone who's loving me.
Go on, now, go!
Walk out the door!
Just turn around now
'Cos you're not welcome any more.
Weren't you the one
who tried to break me with 'goodbye'?
Did you think I'd crumble?
Did you think I'd lay down and die?
Oh no! Not I!
I will survive!
And as long as I know how to love
I know I'll stay alive.
I've got all my life to live
and I've got all my love to give
And I'll survive
I will survive!